Ms Linda Morgan
29 Mount Rock Rd.
Shippensburg, PA 17257-9359

W9-BVZ-585

If anyone is qualified to talk about the "joy of finding Jesus," it is the late Bill Bright.... He was a world-class Christian with a passion for the global glory of God.

From the Foreword by
RICK WARREN

BILL BRIGHT'S
"THE JOY OF KNOWING GOD"
SERIES

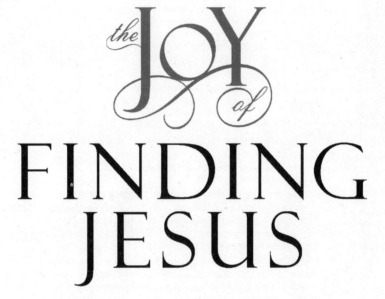

the JOY of
FINDING
JESUS

DR. BILL BRIGHT

The Bible Teacher's Teacher

COOK COMMUNICATIONS MINISTRIES
Colorado Springs, Colorado • Paris, Ontario
KINGSWAY COMMUNICATIONS LTD
Eastbourne, England

Victor® is an imprint of
Cook Communications Ministries,
Colorado Springs, CO 80918
Cook Communications, Paris, Ontario
Kingsway Communications, Eastbourne, England

THE JOY OF FINDING JESUS
© 2005 by Bill Bright

First Printing, 2005
Printed in the United States of America
2 3 4 5 6 7 8 9 10 Printing/Year 09 08 07 06 05

Cover Design: Brand Navigation, LLC

Library of Congress Cataloging-in-Publication Data

Bright, Bill.
  The joy of finding Jesus : he will meet your every need / Bill Bright.
    p. cm. -- (The joy of knowing God series ; bk. 2)
  ISBN 0-7814-4247-8 (pbk.)
  1. Jesus Christ. I. Title. II. Series.

BT203.B76 2005
232--dc22
                                              2004027059

Dedication

GLOBAL FOUNDING PARTNERS

The Bright Media Foundation continues the multifaceted ministries of Bill and Vonette Bright for generations yet unborn. God has touched and inspired the Brights through the ministries of writers through the centuries. Likewise, they wish to pass along God's message in Jesus Christ as they have experienced it, seeking to inspire, train, and transform lives, thereby helping to fulfill the Great Commission each year until our Lord returns.

Many generous friends have prayed and sacrificed to support the Bright Media Foundation's culturally relevant, creative works, in print and electronic forms. The following persons specifically have helped to establish the foundation. These special friends will always be known as Global Founding Partners *of the Bright Media Foundation.*

Bill and Christie Heavener and family

Stuart and Debra Sue Irby and family

Edward E. Haddock Jr., Edye Murphy-Haddock, and the Haddock family

Acknowledgments

It was my privilege to share fifty-four years, six months, and twenty days of married life with a man who loved Jesus passionately and served Him faithfully. Six months before his home going, Bill initiated what has become "The Joy of Knowing God" series. It was his desire to pass along to future generations the insights God had given him that they, too, could discover God's magnificence and live out the wonderful plan He has for their lives.

"The Joy of Knowing God" series is a collection of Bill Bright's top ten life-changing messages. Millions of people around the world have already benefited greatly from these spiritual truths and are now living the exciting Christian adventure that God desires for each of us.

On behalf of Bill, I want to thank the following team that helped research, compile, edit, and wordsmith the manuscripts and audio scripts in this series: Jim Bramlett, Rebecca Cotton, Eric Metaxas, Sheryl Moon, Cecil Price, Michael Richardson, Eric Stanford, and Rob Suggs.

I also want to thank Bill's longtime friends and Campus Crusade associates Bailey Marks and Ted Martin, who carefully reviewed the scripts and manuscripts for accuracy.

Bill was deeply grateful to Bob Angelotti and Don Stillman of Allegiant Marketing Group for their encouragement to produce this series and their ingenuity in facilitating distribution to so many.

A special thanks to Cook Communications and its team of dedicated professionals who partnered with Bright Media Foundation in this venture, as well as to Steve Laube, who brought us together.

Last but not least, I want to express my appreciation to Helmut Teichert, who worked faithfully and diligently in overseeing this team that Bill's vision would be realized, and to John Nill, CEO of Bright Media, who has helped me navigate the many challenges along this journey.

As a result of the hard work of so many, and especially our wonderful Lord's promise of His grace, I trust that multitudes worldwide will experience a greater joy by knowing God and His ways more fully.

With a grateful heart,
MRS. BILL BRIGHT (VONETTE)

Contents

Foreword

If anyone is qualified to talk about the "joy of finding Jesus," it is the late Bill Bright. As founder of Campus Crusade for Christ, Bill created the largest Christian ministry in the world, yet his real legacy is the millions of people he either personally or corporately led to faith in Jesus.

I first met Bill in 1974 while serving as a short-term student missionary to Japan. When I returned to California, I'd often drive to his Arrowhead Springs headquarters to gain wisdom from this spiritual giant. Over the years, our conversations were pivotal in my development as a leader; I will deeply miss his counsel and friendship.

Other than my own father, I can't think of anyone who has influenced me more than Bill Bright. He taught me the power of visionary faith. Bill believed in a big God, so he had big dreams and took big risks. God honored that faith over and over again. Bill taught me that simple tools change the world. Millions of people now have faith in Christ because of his *JESUS* film, *The Four Spiritual Laws* booklet, and more.

I believe no other Christian leader of the twentieth century understood the Great Commission better—or took it more seriously—than Bill Bright. He was a world-class Christian with a passion for the global glory of God. Perhaps the best lesson Bill taught was the power of complete surrender to God. Years ago, I asked, "Why do you think God has used and blessed your life so much?" He told me the story he had told over and over around the world: "When I was a young man, I made a contract with God. I literally wrote it out and signed my name at the bottom. It said, 'From this day forward, I am a slave of Jesus Christ.'"

There may have been few banner headlines announcing the death of Bill Bright, but I am certain that millions upon millions heralded his arrival in heaven.

— RICK WARREN

CHAPTER ONE

The Man Who Changed History

—— ❖ ——

"He who has seen Me has seen the Father."

—Jesus Christ

1

The Man Who Changed History

I would like to ask you a question that I have asked millions of people all over the world—people representing all religions: Who, in your opinion, is the most outstanding personality of all time? Who is the greatest leader? The greatest teacher? Who has done the most good for humankind and lived the most holy life?

Visit any part of the world today; talk to people of any religion—or of no religion. No matter how committed to a particular religion these people may be, if they know anything of the facts, they will have to acknowledge that there has never been a man like Jesus of Nazareth to walk this planet Earth.

Without any doubt, He is the unique personality of all time, a man who changed the course of history so dramatically that almost nothing is untouched by His influence. In almost every country on the globe, the front page of every single newspaper acknowledges Him. That's because every date is marked from His birth more than two thousand years ago.

Hundreds of years before Jesus' birth, Scripture

recorded the words of the great prophets of Israel foretelling His coming. The Old Testament, written by many individuals over a period of fifteen hundred years, contains more than three hundred prophecies detailing His coming, His birth, His death, and His resurrection.

> *The life Jesus led, the miracles He performed, the words He spoke, His death on the cross, His resurrection, His ascent into heaven—these all point to the fact that He was not merely a man but more than a man.*

The life Jesus led, the miracles He performed, the words He spoke, His death on the cross, His resurrection, His ascent into heaven—these all point to the fact that He was not merely a man but more than a man.

In John 10:30 (KJV) Jesus said, "I and my Father are one." And John 14:6 (NKJV) records Jesus as saying, "No one comes to the Father except through Me." He also says, "He who has seen Me has seen the Father" (John 14:9 NKJV).

Those are bold statements! This man was not just a *great* man; He was God incarnate. Who can comprehend such a thing?

Yet trace the life and influence of Jesus Christ and you will observe that His message always effects great change in the lives of people and nations. Wherever His message has gone, slavery has been abolished. Child labor laws have been enacted. Institutions of higher learning have been established. Hospitals have been built. The sanctity of marriage has been acknowledged, as have women's rights. And a multitude of other changes have been made for the good of humankind.

Not only has there been no one like the incomparable Jesus,

but no one else has so dramatically changed so many lives, caused so many revolutions, or impacted so many continents and cultures. The very calendar that guides our days is defined by His brief life; it is based on "the year of our Lord." New lands and great discoveries have come through missionaries seeking to tell others about Him. Social movements, educational advances, and the abolition of slavery have been fueled by men and women changed by this matchless Man of Galilee.

He is clearly the driving force of the last two millennia of this world. Historians will not dispute this. The world was transformed forever on that early morning when His infant cry was first heard in a makeshift manger in an obscure town of a downtrodden and captive nation. Living as a humble peasant, He assumed no throne as an adult—no earthly one, at least— but lived as a man of the people.

Yet the very power of His name was destined to overthrow the most widespread and secure empire the world had ever known, that of the Romans. He never traveled outside the bounds of His own small territory, yet His message would touch every corner of the world. He never wrote a book, yet His words are the best known and most studied of any in the world. Comparatively little is known of His life—only the works and words of a few months from the thirty or so years He lived—yet more books have been written about Him than about any other human being who ever lived.

> *More books have been written about Jesus than about any other human being who ever lived.*

His wonderful light breaks through the darkness of every century and every corner of this world of ours. But sometimes heavenly sunlight is too powerful for human eyes; we evaluate its brilliance by its illumination of all that it touches.

In the same way, we can grasp the greatness of Jesus by examining His impact on particular individuals.

SHINING LIVES

Let me tell you a story. There was a man named Lew Wallace who was both a famous general and a literary genius. He had served as the governor of New Mexico.

General Wallace was also an avowed atheist. One day his friend Robert Ingersoll suggested an idea to the general. Why not write a book proving that no such man as Jesus Christ ever existed? Why not show that Christianity, the world's dominant faith, was completely based on a myth? "It would be a masterpiece," said Ingersoll, "and a way of putting an end to the foolishness about the so-called Christ."

It sounded like a good idea to General Wallace, and he went to the library and began his research. For two years Wallace undertook this ambitious project. He researched and studied in the leading libraries of Europe and America. His goal? To find information that would once and for all destroy Christianity and show it to be the sham that he knew it was.

But something went wrong with his plan. He had written no further than his second chapter when something distressing came to pass. His research did the opposite of what he'd hoped: It actually gave him solid, irrefutable evidence that Jesus Christ was the Son of God. Intellectual integrity forced Wallace to admit that Jesus Christ was just as historical as Julius Caesar or Socrates.

Jesus was *real*; the evidence was clear. And the implications were even more staggering: If this man was indeed genuine, then so was His lordship. He could only be myth or Master, one or the other. There could be no middle ground.

It was clear to Wallace that Jesus Christ was no myth. He fell immediately to his knees and cried out to Jesus, "My Lord and my God!"

"Towards morning the light broke into my soul," he later wrote. "I went into my bedroom, woke my wife, and told her that I had received Jesus Christ as my Lord and Savior." She smiled and told him that this was no less than the answer to her prayer. She had asked God for her husband to be like Saul of Tarsus, who began by casting stones and ended by casting his life before the Savior.

You see, Saul, who became known as Paul the apostle, realized that if people earnestly and honestly sought to get to the bottom of the matter of Jesus Christ, they would inevitably find themselves bowing before Him as Lord. For example, Paul preached to the Bereans, who "listened eagerly to Paul's message. They searched the Scriptures day after day to check up on Paul and Silas, to see if they were really teaching the truth. As a result, many Jews believed, as did some of the prominent Greek women and many men" (Acts 17:11–12).

Why not write a book proving that no such man as Jesus Christ ever existed?

Not only did General Wallace become a Christian, but later in his life, he did indeed write a great book—a masterpiece, just as Ingersoll had predicted. But it was called *Ben-Hur: A Tale of the Christ*. It is a work of beauty and devotion, one of the greatest novels ever written concerning the life and time of Christ, testifying to the Jesus whose acquaintance Wallace had made—the *genuine* Jesus.

There is another true story about a young lawyer named Frank Morison. He set out specifically to disprove the resurrection of Christ. But as he examined the historical evidence, he came to precisely the opposite conclusion. He disposed, one by one, with every theory that could possibly be employed to refute the resurrection. Finally Morison concluded that Christ was risen indeed. For Morison, too, there were implications for his own life that could not be ignored. So he, too, bowed before his Lord and Savior and completed a book very different in premise from the one he had set out to write. It was called *Who Moved the Stone?* It remains to this day a classic and persuasive defense of our Lord's Easter resurrection.

DO WISE MEN STILL SEEK HIM?

When Christ was born, we are told that men from the East traveled a great distance to see the child for themselves and to know the truth. We call them the wise men, and I am happy to say that wise men and women of today still investigate the claims of Jesus. And like those long-ago intellectuals, they bow before Him as Lord.

You see, skeptics could not be more wrong in their assumption that only the unsophisticated follow Christ. It is not true that scientists and scholars must reject any belief in miracles or the supernatural. If they would look a bit deeper into the history of their own fields of research, they would discover that so many of the world's most brilliant men and women have laid their lives before Christ Jesus, who said, "I am the way, the truth, and the life" (John 14:6). Geniuses such as Isaac Newton and Blaise Pascal—founders of entire categories of mathematics and science—knew He was the truth as sure as any equation they could devise.

Similarly the late C. S. Lewis, a professor at Oxford

University, was an avowed agnostic. He denied the deity of Christ for many years. But eventually, he, too, submitted to Jesus as his God and Savior after studying the overwhelming evidence for the deity of Christ. As he came to understand, the Lord had been pursuing him until there was nothing for Lewis to do but to surrender totally. Intellectual honesty required that he admit God must exist. And from there, he felt compelled to follow the logical path of reasoning until he arrived at the conclusion that God could only be known through His Son, Jesus Christ. He then spent much of the rest of his life writing books to help the world come to that same conclusion. In his book *Mere Christianity*, he made this now famous statement:

> A man who is merely a man and said the sort of things Jesus said would not be a great moral teacher. He would either be a lunatic, on the level of a man who says he's a poached egg, or else he would be the Devil of Hell. You must take your choice. Either this was and is the Son of God or else a mad man or something worse. You can shut Him up for a fool, you can spit at Him and kill Him as a demon; or you can fall at His feet and call Him Lord and God. But let us not come up with any patronizing nonsense about His being a great human teacher. He has not left that open to us. He did not intend to.[1]

We have no viable option of dismissing Jesus as an eloquent teacher, as many in our world do. General Wallace and Frank Morison recognized this same principle. He was the Son of God, as He claimed—or else He was someone unworthy of even discussing.

Why? Because He did not simply deliver edifying thoughts

in His teachings. He claimed to be God in the flesh, the Lord of the universe. No merely respectable teacher would say such a thing. There are, therefore, three options for His identity. He was either a lunatic or a liar—or He must, by default, be precisely what He claimed: Lord and Master of creation.

I have yet to meet a person who has honestly considered the overwhelming evidence concerning Jesus of Nazareth who does not admit that He is the Son of God.

John Singleton Copley, recognized as one of the greatest legal minds in British history, made this comment: "I know pretty well what evidence is and I tell you, such evidence as that for the resurrection has never broken down yet."[2]

I have yet to meet a person who has honestly considered the overwhelming evidence concerning Jesus of Nazareth who does not admit that He is the Son of God. Nonbelievers frequently admit they have not taken the time to read the Bible or consider the historical facts concerning Jesus.

General Wallace did so, then put aside his pen and his doubts. Frank Morison's heart became as open as the tomb he had investigated. And C. S. Lewis spent the rest of his life and the vast resources of his intellect helping people clearly perceive the clear truth about Jesus.

In every generation since the first century, people have stood before this man as the crowd in Jerusalem did: "'Tell us who you are,' they demanded. Jesus replied, 'I am the one I have always claimed to be'" (John 8:25).

A TWO-WAY STREET

All creation testifies that Jesus is Lord. Paul wrote, "Christ is the exact likeness of the unseen God. He existed before God made anything at all, and, in fact, Christ himself is the Creator who made everything in heaven and earth" (Colossians 1:15–16 TLB).

We are also given a wonderful hope for the future: "God told us his secret reason for sending Christ, a plan he decided on in mercy long ago; and this was his purpose: that when the time is ripe he will gather us all together from wherever we are—in heaven or on earth—to be with him in Christ, forever" (Ephesians 1:9–10 TLB).

Who is Jesus of Nazareth to you? Your life on this earth and for all eternity is affected by your answer to this question. Take Buddha out of Buddhism, Muhammad out of Islam, and in like manner the founders of various other religions out of their religions, and little would change. But take Jesus Christ out of Christianity and there would be nothing left. You see, Christianity is not a philosophy or an ethic but a personal, dynamic relationship with a living, risen Savior. Anyone who tells you differently is giving you a worthless counterfeit of the real thing. Run from that kind of Christianity. Because without Jesus—the Savior who died for our sins and then rose from the grave and is still alive today—Christianity is worse than nothing.

> *Christianity is not a philosophy or an ethic but a personal, dynamic relationship with a living, risen Savior.*

No other religion claims that its founder has actually been

raised from the dead. Christianity is unique in this regard. And any argument for its validity stands or falls on the resurrection of Jesus of Nazareth. Many great scholars have believed and do believe in His resurrection. After examining the evidence for the resurrection of Jesus given by the gospel writers, the late Simon Greenleaf, an authority in jurisprudence at Harvard Law School, came to this conclusion: "It was therefore impossible that they (referring to the apostles) could have persisted in affirming the truth they've narrated had not Jesus actually risen from the dead and had they not known these facts as certainly as they knew any other fact."[3]

It thrills my soul to tell you that, when you come to know this same Jesus, your life will be totally made new. We are not talking about some empty pattern of religious ritual. Faith in Christ is no religion at all. It is a dynamic, moment-by-moment friendship with the Lord of eternity. Knowing Him is as real as knowing any family member or friend—and far more satisfying to the soul. Because of the resurrection of Jesus, His followers do not merely comply with the ethical code of a dead founder; rather we have vital, dynamic, intimate contact with a living Lord. Jesus Christ lives today and anxiously waits to work in the lives of those who will trust and obey Him.

Indeed Paul said, "To live is Christ" (Philippians 1:21 NKJV). He is everything to me, and I hope He will be everything to you.

I pray that even now, you feel the whisper of God's loving Spirit within you, saying, "Taste and see that the LORD is good. Oh, the joys of those who trust in him!" (Psalm 34:8).

The psalmist also urges you, "Take delight in the LORD, and he will give you your heart's desires. Commit everything you do to the LORD. Trust him, and he will help you" (Psalm 37:4–5).

God's promises are absolute. They are inscribed in the foundations of eternity, for He does not lie. And He has promised you in these two passages that as you taste the infinite joys of the Lord and as you take your delight in Him, the deepest desires of your heart will be met. Can you imagine a more thrilling prospect than that?

You will quickly discover, as I did so many years ago, that to know Jesus is to love Him. As we have seen in this chapter, He is the answer to every question the seeking soul might ask. But we will find that He is much more than that. He and He alone will fill every need of your heart. He and He alone will give you a plan and a purpose for living. And He and He alone is your eternal destiny, as you look to a glorious heavenly life in which you will see Him face-to-face.

THE DISCOVERY OF A LIFETIME

I would ask you, as we close this chapter, to do two things. First, be bold enough to ask the questions, as did the great men we discussed. What questions do you have about Jesus? What doubts or reservations? Write them all down. Keep your questions before you. Since all truth is His truth, no question of yours will bring His kingdom tumbling to the ground. My friend, countless people have tried for two thousand years, and the questioners have joined ranks with those who love our Lord, or they have faded into obscurity. If you would like to investigate the claims of Jesus, I would recommend that you bring your questions to www.jesusfactorfiction.com.

Second, *taste and see*. Seeking the facts is good for the mind, but your heart must also encounter the one and only

Jesus. Claim the two passages from Psalms above. If you are a believer, ask the Lord Jesus Christ to abide in you more deeply than ever before. If you are not, and if your heart and mind agree on His reality and goodness, then chapter 4 will offer you the opportunity to make that decision. Appendix A at the conclusion of this book also gives you the opportunity to examine four compelling spiritual principles that govern our universe. This book is written so that you would meet Jesus and accept Him as your Lord and Savior.

Let us set about on that journey, seeking the great discovery of a lifetime, the Friend who will redefine everything about you. It is my pleasure to introduce to you the most powerful Lord and wonderful Companion any man, woman, or child will ever have: the one and only Lord Jesus Christ.

---

1. C. S. Lewis, *Mere Christianity* (New York: The Macmillian Company, 1960), pp. 40–41.

2. Quoted in Wilbur M. Smith, *Therefore Stand* (Boston: W. A. Wilde Company, 1945), p. 425.

3. Simon Greenleaf, *The Testimony of the Evangelists Examined by the Rules of Evidence Administered in Courts of Justice* (Newark, NJ: Soney & Sage, 1903).

CHAPTER TWO

A Friend for Every Season

——————❖——————

GOD THE FATHER TELLS US THAT THOSE WHO
DEMONSTRATE LOVE FOR HIS SON ARE
HEIRS TO HIS KINGDOM.

————————————

A Friend for Every Season

The story is told of a very wealthy old man who passed away. A large contingent of friends and relatives gathered for his funeral. Though he was a warmhearted and generous man, he was surrounded by hangers-on who were more interested in his possessions than his person. This is too often the case with men and women of material wealth.

There was great speculation and debate about the future of the estate, for it seemed that the old man had died without a last will and testament. You can well imagine the conflicts and heated words that were exchanged. This son had his lawyer, this daughter had hers, and these relatives had their own claims to assert. The house was filled with antiques and art treasures, and every claimant seemed to have a special target. The whole disruptive mess was relegated to the legal system. All the treasures and furnishings of the great mansion were divided and removed. The wealth was dispensed in a number of directions.

When nearly everything was gone and the mansion was a near shell, a shy, elderly nurse turned up to make a modest request. She asked for a dusty, neglected old portrait of the man's eldest son. He had been a son the nurse had helped raise from infancy, a son who had died years ago in war. She treasured the young man's memory and wanted his picture.

No one else seemed to care about the old canvas; it had no market value. So the nurse received her permission. But as the picture was being dismounted from the parlor wall, a bulge was noticed in the canvas. The curious executor looked behind the frame and discovered the old man's missing will! It happened to be a very simple one: The old man had wanted *all of his estate* to go to the person who demonstrated love and affection for his son—whoever that person might be—through claiming this portrait. Only that person would discover the will of the departed patriarch.

Our world is much like that estate with its squabbling scavengers and treasure hunters. We spend our time and energy competing for things that will not last. Meanwhile God the Father tells us that those who demonstrate love for His Son are heirs to His

God loves us with an everlasting love—a forever love—and pursues our affection relentlessly.

kingdom. They will discover the wonderful will of the Father.

Jesus, His Son, is our way to that Father who has loved us from the beginning. We were specifically created to share in a wonderful friendship with Him—to be His children and the heirs to His kingdom. He has said, "I have loved you, my people, with an everlasting love. With unfailing love I have drawn you to myself" (Jeremiah 31:3). Most amazing and wonderful of all, He has loved us through all of our sin, all of our rebellion, regardless of every deed you and I have undertaken, one after another, to break His loving heart.

Even now He loves us with an *everlasting* love—a forever love—and pursues our affection relentlessly. To show us once and for all just how deep and how wide is His love for us, He sent His own Son as the very image of himself in the flesh, a living portrait of a God whose magnificence, holiness, and all-consuming power overwhelm and transcend all human understanding. Jesus explained this to His disciples: "I am the way, the truth, and the life. No one can come to the Father except through me. If you had known who I am, then you would have known who my Father is. From now on you know him and have seen him!" (John 14:6–7).

Any serious disciple of our Lord will read the Word prayerfully each day and focus on the Gospels regularly.

KNOWING JESUS

But this is the good news—we *can* know who Jesus is. We can know Him through His Word, preserved for us in the Holy Scriptures; and we can know Him through His Spirit, sent to indwell us, to guide us, and to nurture us spiritually.

The first way you can get to know Jesus is to read at least one of the four biographies of Him in the inspired Word of God. Even if you have been His follower for many years, I strongly suggest you take some time to do this. Any serious disciple of our Lord will read the Word prayerfully each day and focus on the Gospels regularly. If you are new to Jesus, I recommend that you start with the wonderful gospel of John—the fourth of those four books. John was a young man who knew and followed his Master. Many years later he wrote this account for us.

As you become better acquainted with God's eternal Son, you will be struck with several remarkable characteristics of His personality. I wish to point out six of them in this chapter.

HIS COMMONNESS

Perhaps the very first trait we notice about Jesus is that He was "one of us." Yes, He was the King of Glory, the eternal Son of God. He was present at the creation of this world. And yet He made His entrance not as a conquering emperor, but as a helpless peasant child. Born and raised in the humblest of circumstances, it was He, "who, being in very nature God, did not consider equality with God something to be grasped, but made himself nothing, taking the very nature of a servant, being made in human likeness" (Philippians 2:6–7 NIV).

Jesus might have selected anyone in the world to follow Him. Yet again, He called *common* men: fishermen, businessmen, plain folks. Many of His followers were women, even though women were often treated very poorly in that time and culture. He loved children, and they returned His affections.

Jesus walked among ordinary people with an extraordinary love.

When some of Jesus' followers tried to restrain the youngsters from clustering around Him, our Lord said, "Let the little children come to me, and do not hinder them, for the kingdom of heaven belongs to such as these" (Matthew 19:14 NIV).

It was farmers and fishermen who listened so intently to the teachings of Jesus. He placed His uncommon teachings in common packages, speaking of planting and casting nets, of working in vineyards, of holding wedding celebrations. In every way, Jesus was one of us.

HIS COMPASSION

Jesus walked among ordinary people with an extraordinary love. "When he saw the crowds, he had compassion on them, because they were harassed and helpless, like sheep without a shepherd" (Matthew 9:36 NIV). He looked out among the masses of people—many of them suffering from diseases, many of them filthy, many of them loud and demanding immediate attention—and He had compassion for them.

Is it not still true today? There is so much about us that is not ideal. We have problems of all kinds, and we are stubborn and slow to become wise and mature. Yet Jesus looks upon you and me and feels nothing but love and the desire to make us whole. Two thousand years ago, the crowds came into His presence and knew immediately how much He cared for them.

At the dawn of His earthly ministry, just before He was ready to introduce himself and His work, He showed this evidence of the heart within Him:

> A man with leprosy came to him and begged him on his knees, "If you are willing, you can make me clean."
>
> Filled with compassion, Jesus reached out his hand and touched the man. "I am willing," he said. "Be clean!" Immediately the leprosy left him and he was cured.
>
> Jesus sent him away at once with a strong warning: "See that you don't tell this to anyone. But go, show yourself to the priest and offer the sacrifices that Moses commanded for your cleansing, as a testimony to them."
>
> MARK 1:40–44 NIV

Imagine that! The Son of God, carrying out a divine agenda set in the very foundations of eternity, improvised His program on the spot. He set aside His timetable to respond to a sick man who needed Him. That is the Jesus we love and the Jesus who *is* love incarnate. John tells us that "God is love" (1 John 4:8, 16), and that quality, more than any other, summarizes Him for us.

As you get to know Jesus, never forget for an instant that He is the ultimate manifestation of love and compassion—and *you* are the object of these. No one will ever adore you as He does.

HIS COMPANIONSHIP

It stands to reason that One with perfect compassion would be perfect in friendship. For a man who seldom stayed in one place for long, Jesus had a remarkable number of close friends. There were His disciples, of course. But He was also close to people such as Mary, Martha, and Lazarus, in whose home He was often a guest. Jesus wept at the death of His good friend Lazarus before returning him to life (see John 11). The Gospels are filled with references to the friends of Jesus, and He was even bitterly accused of being "a friend of sinners"! Praise God, He is indeed the perfect friend for sinners like you and me.

Jesus made His greatest statement about friendship to His disciples, just before His arrest by the Romans and His trial: "The greatest love is shown when people lay down their lives for their friends. You are my friends if you obey me. I no longer call you servants, because a master doesn't confide in his servants. Now you are my friends, since I have told you everything the Father told me" (John 15:13–15).

Remember, this is the very image of our loving Father; this is God in the flesh. And He insists on calling us His friends rather than His servants, teaching us all about our heavenly Father as we obey Him in love and faith—a perfect picture of the wonderful friendship we enjoy together. *What a friend we have in Jesus.*

HIS CONSECRATION

Consecration is a lovely old word that means "set apart for God's use." Jesus was our ultimate example of such dedication. Before His birth, angels visited both His parents and instructed that He be committed completely to the purposes of His heavenly Father. By the time He was twelve, Jesus was at the temple in Jerusalem, teaching the wisest of the rabbis there. At the outset of His ministry, He traveled alone into the desert for prayer and fasting, committing himself wholly to God's purposes.

Even as the crowds pressed in, making their demands, and even as He served as the perfect friend with the perfect compassion—even then He remained fully dedicated to communion with the Lord. We are told that

What a friend we have in Jesus.

"Jesus awoke long before daybreak and went out alone into the wilderness to pray" (Mark 1:35). Finally, knowing that a cruel death sentence awaited Him, He went to the garden of Gethsemane to recommit himself, even at pain of death. As human as you or me, He struggled: "If it is possible, let this cup of suffering be taken away from me. Yet I want your will, not mine" (Matthew 26:39).

Not only is Jesus perfect in His devotion to you; He is perfect in His devotion to God.

HIS COMMAND

We cannot discuss the wonderful nature of our Lord Jesus Christ without mentioning His awesome power, even as One who submitted himself to human form and to death. Jesus spoke with the full authority and power of His Father. At His word, diseases were cured and demons fled. At His command, storms subsided. The disciples, in awe of His power, said, "Who is this man, that even the wind and waves obey him?" (Mark 4:41). At His bidding, death itself departed from Lazarus and two others who had died (John 11; Luke 7:11–17; Luke 8:49–56).

When Jesus faced His terrible crucifixion, He stood silent before Roman procurator Pontius Pilate, who asked, "Don't you realize that I have the power to release you or to crucify you?" Jesus replied, "You would have no power over me at all unless it were given to you from above" (John 19:10–11). Jesus knew that His own power and authority came from above—as does all power and all authority; our God is in control. Yet Jesus submitted to death because we could only be saved from our sin by someone who had humanity in *common* with us; by someone with the ultimate *compassion* and *companionship;* by someone fully *consecrated* to God, capable of *commanding* death itself to retreat; and finally, someone willing to take such a heavenly mission to *completion.*

HIS COMPLETION

Your Lord and Savior and mine, Jesus Christ, finished the task He set out to do. When we could not be reconciled to the Father any other way, He came on a rescue mission to first show us what God was like, then show us the breadth of God's love, then demonstrate the depth of His awesome power by rising from the dead. We have already seen the great words of Philippians 2 that tell us how He humbled himself to take the form of a man. But that would not have been enough to break the power of sin if He had not been fully dedicated to what the task required:

> And in human form he obediently humbled himself even further by dying a criminal's death on a cross. Because of this, God raised him up to the heights of heaven and gave him a name that is above every other name, so that at the name of Jesus every knee will bow, in heaven and on earth and under the earth, and every tongue will confess that Jesus Christ is Lord, to the glory of God the Father.
>
> PHILIPPIANS 2:8–11

I hope you now see just what kind of friend we have in Jesus—Someone who was one of us, Someone compassionate and caring and companionable, yes. But He was also Someone who commanded the wind and the seas, who broke the power of death, and who sits at the right hand of the Father in heaven, where someday every knee will bow before His magnificence. He is the complete Lord for us, the complete Savior from our sin, the complete answer to every need we have, as we will see.

Jesus is the complete Lord for us, the complete Savior from our sin, the complete answer to every need we have.

More books have been written about this humble carpenter, this all-powerful Lord and Savior, than anyone who ever lived. So neither this brief chapter nor this slim volume can possibly do justice to the goal of presenting Him to you in all His perfection. No book could do that. But there is a better way.

I have already recommended that you carefully read the gospel of John—or one of the other three accounts of the life of Jesus. In this way you will meet Him with your mind. But with all that is within me, I urge you to meet Him with your heart as well by coming into His presence. Jesus said, "'You must love the Lord your God with all your heart, all your soul, and all your mind.' This is the first and greatest commandment" (Matthew 22:37–38).

It is also my first and greatest prayer for you. Meet Jesus. Meet Him today, with all that is within you. Spend time talking to Him, just as you would talk with anyone else. Tell Him all your hopes and dreams. Ask Him to walk with you through each moment of your life. He will answer that prayer, and He will fill your every need—which brings us to our next chapter.

CHAPTER THREE

A Gift for Every Need

---·---

"So do not fear, for I am with you;
do not be dismayed, for I am your God. I will
strengthen you and help you; I will uphold you
with my righteous right hand."

Isaiah 41:10 NIV

3

A Gift for Every Need

The human soul has three fundamental desires. God's satisfaction of these three deep longings provides the foundation for true peace and joy in our lives. The first desire is for unconditional love and total acceptance; the second is for absolute and eternal security; and the third is for a sense of significance, that our lives really and truly matter.

Most of us have noticed that it is possible to gain the whole world without satisfying these needs of the soul.

Billy Joel became one of the most successful recording artists in the world. At the height of his career he won awards for Male Artist of the Year, Record of the Year, Song of the Year, and Album of the Year. During the 1980s he managed to enjoy twenty Top 40 hits. As his crowning musical achievement, he was inducted into the Rock and Roll Hall of Fame. But in a recent interview, Joel admitted that he had never found fulfillment.

Baseball player Pete Rose reached one of the most coveted milestones of his sport: He recorded more base hits than any player in history. But the Baseball Hall of Fame, in

Cooperstown, New York, refused to enshrine him. Why? Because it was proved that he was guilty of betting on baseball games. After fourteen years of denials, he finally admitted to the charge in his book *My Prison Without Bars*. He, too, confessed to despair of an empty life.

Both singer and slugger discovered that wealth, fame, and success cannot deliver the happiness they promise.

Joel said, "In my whole life, I haven't met the person I can sustain a relationship with yet … I'm angry with myself. I have regrets." Both Joel's marriages ended in divorce. "You don't get hugged by the Rock and Roll Hall of Fame," he said ruefully. "I want what everybody else wants: to love and to be loved, and to have a family."[1]

> *All history and all the world form together one great testimony to the human heart and its constant, desperate pursuit of fulfillment.*

Rose, who lost hundreds of thousands of dollars through gambling, declared, "A part of me was still looking for ways to recapture the high I got from winning batting titles and World Series. If I couldn't get the high from playing baseball, then I needed a substitute to keep from feeling depressed. I was driven, in gambling as well as in baseball. Enough was never enough. I had huge appetites, and I was always hungry."[2]

How many more examples could you or I add to these two? All history and all the world form together one great testimony to the human heart and its constant, desperate pursuit of fulfillment. Everywhere we go, we find that people are basically the same; they have the same needs, the same desires, and the same anger and despair when they cannot fulfill them. In Western nations, our culture leads us to believe that material attainments can satisfy us—that if we simply collect enough wealth, we will be happy. Yet not only is there no evidence of that assertion, but all the evidence points to the opposite conclusion. When the needs of the soul are ignored, misery and money escalate together because wealth becomes a master rather than a servant; it uses us rather than the other way around.

How blessed we are to discover that those needs can be met, even if the world has no resources to meet them. Jesus— the wonderful Jesus whose personality and power we explored in the preceding chapter—will fill our every need. And in particular, He will fill the three needs shared by every human being. Let us discover what these are.

LOVE WITHOUT LIMITS

The first desire is for unconditional love and acceptance. This is something that every person seeks. But we don't just want it from anyone; we tend to want it from those people who matter most in our eyes.

So most of us go about trying to gain the approval of those people, whether they are our parents, our bosses, or people we want to impress in order to be part of their social circle.

But that kind of love and acceptance is totally conditional; it depends on what we may or may not do. What's more, the people whose approval we are trying to gain might themselves have skewed values. So we might spend years and decades trying to gain the approval of someone or some group whose approval may even be directly contrary to what God wants.

Only God can offer us truly unconditional love and acceptance forever. Only by seeking His approval do we know we are headed in the right direction.

Unlike people, God loves us no matter how we perform. Even when we make mistakes, He is on our side, rooting for us. If the God of the universe loves us and is cheering for us, why would we care what others think of us? God's Word tells us,

---❖---

Unlike people, God loves us no matter how we perform.

If God is for us, who can ever be against us? Since God did not spare even his own Son but gave him up for us all, won't God, who gave us Christ, also give us everything else?

Who dares accuse us whom God has chosen for his own? Will God? No! He is the one who has given us right standing with himself. Who then will condemn us? Will Christ Jesus? No, for he is the one who died for us and was raised to life for us and is sitting at the place of highest honor next to God, pleading for us.

Can anything ever separate us from Christ's love? Does it mean he no longer loves us if we have trouble or calamity, or are persecuted, or are hungry or cold or in danger or threatened with death? … No, despite all these things, overwhelming victory is ours through Christ, who loved us.

And I am convinced that nothing can ever separate us from his love. Death can't, and life can't. The angels can't, and the demons can't. Our fears for today, our worries about tomorrow, and even the powers of hell can't keep God's love away. Whether we are high above the sky or in the deepest ocean, nothing in all creation will ever be able to separate us from the love of God that is revealed in Christ Jesus our Lord.

Now that's real unconditional love and acceptance. If God loves us as we are and forgives us any failings, who has the right to condemn us? No one! God himself sent Jesus to die for us because of how much He loves us and wants us to be with Him forever. Whose approval could ever matter more than His? Who can ever keep that kind of love away from us?

The best news is that you need not give anything but your heart. Jesus is the One who has done the giving. He gave His life to bring you that love.

Blessed Assurance

The second deep desire each person has is for security. And to find the security we want, we try to obtain what we believe will meet our future needs. But how do we know what to prepare for? We can spend a lifetime accumulating riches and feel secure only to have it all wiped out in a stock-market crash, a fire, or an illness.

Only God knows the future, and only He can offer us genuine security. Remember this story from the twelfth chapter of the gospel of Luke?

> The ground of a certain rich man produced a good crop.
> He thought to himself, "What shall I do? I have no place to store my crops."
> Then he said, "This is what I'll do. I will tear down my barns and build bigger ones, and there I will store all my grain and my goods. And I'll say to myself, 'You have plenty of good things laid up for many years. Take life easy; eat, drink and be merry.'"

But God said to him, "You fool! This very night your life will be demanded from you. Then who will get what you have prepared for yourself?"

This is how it will be with anyone who stores up things for himself but is not rich toward God.

VERSES 16–21 NIV

And Proverbs 3:25–26 (NIV) says, "Have no fear of sudden disaster or of the ruin that overtakes the wicked, for the LORD will be your confidence and will keep your foot from being snared."

If we find our security in Jesus, we have absolutely nothing to fear. He knows the future and will be with us in all circumstances. In Isaiah 41:10 (NIV) God promises, "So do not fear, for I am with you; do not be dismayed, for I am your God. I will strengthen you and help you; I will uphold you with my righteous right hand."

Only God knows the future, and only He can offer us genuine security.

To build your life on the person of Christ is to be (in His own words) "like a person who builds a house on solid rock. Though the rain comes in torrents and the floodwaters rise and the winds beat against that house, it won't collapse, because it is built on rock" (Matthew 7:24–25). Others build their houses on the sand of wealth, fame, or power. At any moment, all they have built may be swept away like sand castles before a stormy sea.

In the words of the old hymn, we can say, "Blessed assurance! Jesus is mine!" It is the ultimate assurance. When you find it, peace will flood through you. You will feel, once again, like that little child climbing into the lap of an all-powerful, all-protecting Father. You will sleep deeply and feel wonderful refreshment in the depths of your soul.

Real security—true security—only comes in Jesus Christ.

SUPREME SIGNIFICANCE

The third deep desire that every person has is for significance—for doing something with our lives that is of lasting value and impact, something that really matters, that makes our lives worth having lived.

Many of us try to do things that seem to be important in the eyes of others, but how can we know that what we are doing with our lives has *real* significance?

How can we know if all our efforts will end up being misguided? Will we have spent our entire lives climbing what we thought was the ladder of success only later to discover that it was leaning against the wrong wall? First Corinthians 3:11–15 (TLB) makes it clear that God is the judge of what is eternally significant and what is merely temporary. The apostle Paul explains:

> And no one can ever lay any other real foundation than that one we already have—Jesus Christ. But there are various kinds of materials that can be used to build on that foundation. Some use gold and silver and jewels; and some build with sticks, and hay, or even straw! There is going to come a time of testing at Christ's Judgment Day to see what kind of material each builder has used. Everyone's work will be put through the fire so that all can see whether or not it keeps its value, and what was really accomplished. Then every workman who has built on the foundation with the right materials, and whose

work still stands, will get his pay. But if the house he has built burns up, he will have a great loss. He himself will be saved, but like a man escaping through a wall of flames.

Only work done for God will last. And only by having a vital relationship with Jesus can we know what God wants us to do with our lives—what work He has chosen for us.

We invest ourselves in many directions, but only when, as Jesus said, "you live for him and make the Kingdom of God your primary concern" (Matthew 6:33) will you feel that your life counts for all that your Lord intended it to count for. Only those things that you dedicate to eternity will last—and you find out what they are by meeting Jesus.

Friend, could you be that hurting person whose needs are not being met by the world's counterfeit solutions? Have you felt unloved, insecure, insignificant? I invite you today to retrace the steps that have brought you to this place in your life. Consider carefully each of these three issues, and apply the truths about them to your life.

> *Only those things that you dedicate to eternity will last—and you find out what they are by meeting Jesus.*

Where have you sought love—or what have you sought in its place?

How have you tried to find security—and how much peace and rest have resulted?

What are you doing to make your life significant—and what difference is your life making?

My recommendation is that you divide a sheet of paper into three columns and begin to truthfully answer these questions. Ask God to point you to the truth. Jesus promised that His Spirit "leads into all truth" (John 14:17).

Then, after you have worked through a frank evaluation of your life, your needs, and how you have met them, I ask you to spend time with Jesus himself, praying about each gift that only He can provide. You need not plead with Him; I assure you that He longs to give even more than you long to accept.

My Lord Jesus Christ wants to fill your every need. When you allow Him to do so, you will find perfect, unconditional love; absolute security; eternal significance—all of them overflowing in abundance to everyone you know.

---

1. http://seattlepi.nwsource.com/people/87390_people18.shtml Seattle News Sept. 18, 2002.

2. http://abclocal.go.com/ktrk/sports/010504_APsports_rosé.html.

———————❖———————

JESUS SUFFERED AND DIED ON YOUR BEHALF,
THEN ROSE TO YOUR ETERNAL BENEFIT.
BUT IT IS NOT ENOUGH JUST TO KNOW AND
BELIEVE THESE TRUTHS. WE MUST ACT ON THEM.

————————————

CHAPTER FOUR

A Decision for Every Life

---❖---

YET TO ALL WHO RECEIVED HIM,
TO THOSE WHO BELIEVED IN HIS NAME, HE GAVE THE
RIGHT TO BECOME CHILDREN OF GOD.

JOHN 1:12 NIV

4

A Decision for Every Life

Blaise Pascal was a famous French physicist and philoso-
pher. He wrote that there is a God-shaped vacuum in
the heart of every person that only God can fill
through His Son, Jesus Christ.

Would you like to know Jesus Christ personally? You can.
As incredible as it may sound, Jesus is so eager to establish a
loving relationship with you that He has already made all the
arrangements. The major barrier that prevents anyone from
enjoying this relationship is ignorance of who Jesus is and what
He has done for us.

I pray that you will be able to discover the joyful reality of
knowing Jesus personally. Nothing is more important, nothing
is more glorious, and nothing is more real.

How to Know God Personally

This chapter's four principles will help you to discover how
to know God personally and experience the abundant life
He promised. As you read them, consider that at this very
moment, there is no reason in heaven or earth that you cannot

accept this wonderful gift. In Revelation 3:20, Jesus implores you, "Look! Here I stand at the door and knock. If you hear me calling and open the door, I will come in, and we will share a meal as friends."

Can you envision that image—Jesus at the door of your life, asking to come in? It is so powerful, so compelling, that the artist Holman Hunt painted it on canvas. The picture is a beloved classic, *The Light of the World*. The Savior's face is kind and eager. The door is covered with ivy, telling us it has not been opened in some time. Then we look closer and realize the door has no knob, no handle by which someone could enter from the outside.

Our Lord never forces His way into the domain of the human heart. Instead He stands gently knocking. We must open that door and allow Him to come in. Why are we so reluctant to open the door for the loving Lord of the universe, to invite him in to "share a meal as friends"?

A little boy may have had the answer. When his father showed him the painting and explained its meaning, he asked why there was no sign of the resident inviting Jesus in. The father had no answer. The boy thought a while and said, "Perhaps they never heard His knock. Perhaps they were spending their time in the cellar."

That little boy may have had a valuable insight. What a tragedy that someone could become so involved in the cellar of his life—with the dust and the refuse of this world—that he misses the gentle knock of the Savior, yearning to know him better.

I pray that you have heard His voice and felt the gentle rhythm of His hand rapping at the door of your soul. The door only opens one way, and it must be opened by you. I wish to offer you four principles to help you do so and to enjoy the wonderful fellowship that Jesus offers us.

GOD LOVES US DEEPLY AND MADE US TO LOVE HIM

The Bible declares in John 3:16 (NKJV): "God so loved the world that He gave His only begotten Son, that whoever believes in Him should not perish but have everlasting life." Because God loves us, He wants us to live our lives with Him—both now and for all eternity. That is His plan. As Jesus expresses in John 17:3: "And this is the way to have eternal life—to know you, the only true God, and Jesus Christ, the one you sent to earth."

You came into this world to love and serve your Father. Jesus came into this world to bring you home, after you (with the rest of humanity) had

> *Human beings were created to have fellowship with God.*

gone astray. We are each of us like the lost son in Luke 15:11–32. We wandered far away from our true home—His kingdom—and squandered all He had given us. Like the father in the story, God waited patiently for us to return, with love and compassion rather than anger. But He did more than wait. He sent His Son into the world, as John 3:16 tells us.

Our Father simply will not give us up, for His plans for us are far too wonderful. He wants us to live forever. He wants us to live more abundantly now. He yearns for us to be heirs of all the joy and all the delights of His kingdom. Oh, how He loves us. Oh, what life can be when we love Him, too.

But there is a problem: a terrible obstruction that separates us from that loving Father.

WE ARE SINFUL AND SEPARATED FROM GOD

In Romans 3:23 (NIV) the Bible explains: "All have sinned and fall short of the glory of God." Human beings were created to have fellowship with God. But because of our own stubborn self-will, we chose to go our own independent way. As a result, fellowship with God was broken.

This self-will, characterized by an attitude of active rebellion or passive indifference, is evidence of what the Bible calls sin. We are also separated from God. Romans 6:23 (NIV) states: "The wages of sin is death." This death means more than a heart ceasing to beat or the loss of brain activity. The Bible here is speaking of a death in a relationship—spiritual separation from our creator God.

Second Thessalonians 1:8–9 (NIV) offers these solemn words: "He will punish those who do not know God and do not obey the gospel of our Lord Jesus. They will be punished with everlasting destruction and shut out from the presence of the Lord." You see, God is a holy God and people are sinful; a great gulf separates the two. By striving to live a good life, studying philosophy, or adhering to some religion, we continually try to reach God and establish a personal relationship with Him through our own efforts. But inevitably we fail.

The gulf is far greater than anything we could ever bridge on our own. Try to imagine a sinless day. If you have an accurate understanding of sin, you will know that you can hardly even imagine it, let alone live that way. The biblical word for *sin*, in its original connotation, means "missing the mark." It is more than simply breaking obvious laws. Anything we do *or think* that is short of God's perfect standards is sin.

Within you, my friend, there is active rebellion and passive resistance. Both of these controlling attitudes are the fruit of sin. There is nothing you can do by yourself to wipe all the stain of sin from your life. It would be like using a teacup to bail water from a sinking ship. Sin rushes in like the raging sea, overwhelming us in our weak moral state.

And remember, the least trace of sin disqualifies us from coming into the presence of a holy God. Our God is light, and in Him is no darkness at all (see 1 John 1:5). Therefore, in the end, all darkness is naturally driven away by the power and brightness of light.

How, then, do we deal with the problem of this darkness within us? Looking at it another way, how do we bridge the great chasm that separates us from our loving Father?

JESUS IS GOD'S BRIDGE FOR REUNITING US WITH HIM

Jesus Christ is God's only provision for people's sin. Through Him alone we can know God personally and experience God's love. Why? First, He died in our place. Romans 5:8 (KJV) tells us, "God commendeth his love toward us, in that, while we were yet sinners, Christ died for us."

God himself has bridged the gulf that separates us from Him by sending His Son, Jesus Christ, to die on the cross in our place to pay the penalty for our sins.

Second, He rose from the dead. The Bible explains in 1 Corinthians 15:3–6: "Christ died for our sins, just as the Scriptures said. He was buried, and he was raised from the dead on the third day, as the Scriptures said. He was seen by Peter and then by the twelve apostles. After that, he was seen by more than five hundred of his followers at one time."

What an amazing truth that Jesus Christ, because He is God, conquered death and separation from God by rising from the dead. Truly He is the only way to God. Jesus declared, as recorded in John 14:6, "I am the way, the truth, and the life. No one can come to the Father except through me." God himself has bridged the gulf that separates us from Him by sending His Son, Jesus Christ, to die on the cross in our place to pay the penalty for our sins.

Again it is Paul who explains: "For sin is the sting that results in death, and the law gives sin its power. How we thank God, who gives us victory over sin and death through Jesus Christ our Lord!" (1 Corinthians 15:56–57).

Jesus suffered and died on your behalf, then rose to your eternal benefit. But it is not enough just to know and believe these truths. We must act on them.

WE MUST INDIVIDUALLY RECEIVE CHRIST AS SAVIOR AND LORD

John 1:12 says, "Yet to all who received him, to those who believed in his name, he gave the right to become children of God" (NIV). How incredible that—not only can we know God personally—we can become His children through faith in Jesus Christ!

You see, it is *faith*, not our own efforts to be good. Faith alone is the key. It is purely through faith that we receive Jesus as our Savior and Lord and are adopted into God's family. The Bible explains in Ephesians 2:8–9 (NASB): "By grace you have been saved through faith; and that not of yourselves, it is the gift of God; not as a result of works, so that no one may boast."

When we receive Jesus Christ, we experience a new birth. Jesus declares, "Unless one is born again, he cannot see the kingdom of God" (John 3:3 NKJV). Because of Jesus we can be forgiven, cleansed, and begin anew as children of God, but we must receive Christ by a personal invitation. Remember the painting of Christ at the door? "… If anyone hears My voice and opens the door, I will come in to him" (Revelation 3:20 NKJV).

Jesus stands at the door of our intellect, our emotions, and our will. Opening the door and receiving Him involves repenting, which simply means turning away from ourselves and our selfishness; turning to God, totally; and asking Jesus Christ to come into our lives to forgive our sins and to make us what He wants us to be.

Just to agree intellectually that Jesus Christ is the Son of God and that He died on the cross for our sin is not enough. Nor is it enough to have an emotional experience. We receive Christ by faith as an act of our will.

WHO IS ON THE THRONE?

I would like for you to envision a circle representing your life. Inside this circle, picture a throne—a place of control. I will describe this life as a self-directed life with self in control of the life. Christ is outside, and all the person's interests are directed by self, resulting in discord and frustration.

Now picture a similar circle. This one I will describe as a Christ-directed life. In this life Christ is on the throne, and the self is yielded to Him. As a result, the person's interests are directed by Jesus, resulting in harmony with God's plan.

Now I want to ask you a very important question: *Which one of these two circles best represents your life?* Which circle would you like to have represent your life? You can literally enter into a personal relationship with God, your heavenly Father, by receiving Christ right now by faith through prayer. Yes, it really is that simple! The Bible makes it very clear. Prayer is simply talking with God, and God knows your heart.

He is not so concerned with your words as He is with the attitude inside your heart. If you sincerely desire for Christ to come into your life right now, I invite you to pray the following prayer:

> Lord Jesus, I want to know You personally. Thank You for dying on the cross for my sins. I surrender the throne of my life to You, and I receive You as my Savior and Lord. Thank You for forgiving my sins and giving me eternal life. Take control of the throne of my life. Make me the kind of person You want me to be. Amen.

Did you pray that prayer? If so, I'm certain you meant it. According to God's promise in Revelation 3:20, where is Christ right now in relation to you? Jesus said that He would come into your life and be your friend, your Savior, your Lord, your Master, so that you can know Him personally. Would He mislead you?

The promise of God's Word, not our feelings, is our authority.

On what authority do you know that God has answered your prayer? It is on the trustworthiness of God himself and His holy Word. The Bible promises eternal life to all who receive Him. In 1 John 5:11–13 (NASB), we read, "And the testimony is this, that God has given us eternal life, and this life is in His Son. He who has the Son has the life; he who does not have the Son of God does not have the life. These things I have written to you who believe in the name of the Son of God, so that you may know that you have eternal life."

And the Scriptures record that God will never leave you;

He declares in Hebrews 13:5 (NASB), "I will never desert you, nor will I ever forsake you."

If you prayed that prayer and meant it, thank God right now that Christ is in your life. Thank Him that on the basis of His promise, you have eternal life from the very moment you invite Him in. He will not deceive you.

Finally, I must urge you: Do not depend on your feelings. The promise of God's Word, not our feelings, is our authority. The Christian lives by faith in the trustworthiness of God himself and His holy Word.

Nothing in the entire world could be more wonderful than Christ inviting you to share the adventure with Him—nothing, that is, except your acceptance of His invitation. But there is more! As we come to know Jesus, the good news keeps coming. In the next chapter we learn about the wonderfully abundant everyday life that He intends for us.

———————— ❖ ————————

ISN'T IT EXCITING TO KNOW THAT, EVEN THOUGH WE ARE
SURROUNDED BY EVIL IN THIS WORLD, WE ARE FREE FROM
ITS POWER? STILL, THIS IS A FREEDOM WE MUST *CLAIM*.

————————————————

CHAPTER FIVE

A Purpose for Every Moment

---◆---

BUT NOW YOU ARE FREE FROM THE POWER OF SIN
AND HAVE BECOME SLAVES OF GOD. NOW YOU
DO THOSE THINGS THAT LEAD TO HOLINESS
AND RESULT IN ETERNAL LIFE.

ROMANS 6:22

5

A Purpose for Every Moment

Christian doesn't live life in half measures, merely trying to be a good person. Faith in Jesus is infinitely more than that!

Jesus intended the Christian life to be an exciting, abundant adventure. He promised, "I have come that [you] may have life, and have it to the full" (John 10:10 NIV).

When you walk in a close relationship with our Lord, and under the control of God's Holy Spirit, every day is filled with wonder, meaning, and purpose—your life overflows with desirable qualities. The Scripture says that "the fruit of the Spirit is love, joy, peace, patience, kindness, goodness, faithfulness, gentleness and self-control" (Galatians 5:22–23 NIV).

But many Christians don't experience this abundant life. The life of joy and victory modeled and promised by our Lord is strangely foreign to them. Instead, they consider the Christian life a burden, a chore—a terrible cross to bear. They endure their Christianity on earth, hoping at last for relief in heaven.

But Jesus never intended for you to live a defeated, dreary

existence. He called you to a life of joy and victory. Whatever your circumstances—comfort or conflict, abundance or need, health or sickness, freedom or persecution—our Lord promises peace (John 14:27; 16:33). He said that He would never leave you and that He will do anything you ask in His name (Hebrews 13:5; Matthew 28:20; John 14:14).

Whatever your circumstances—comfort or conflict, abundance or need, health or sickness, freedom or persecution—our Lord promises peace.

The simple fact is this: God created each human being with psychological needs that only God himself can satisfy. When we try to satisfy those needs outside of God, we will always fail, but when we look to Him first, our desires are met in ways we never imagined. Psalm 37:4 promises, "Take delight in the LORD, and he will give you your heart's desires."

I wonder whether we truly realize what it means to find delight in our wonderful Lord. Campus Crusade for Christ International has shown the film called *JESUS* to billions of people across the globe, and we have seen firsthand what it is like when people experience that delight for the first time. Through the showing of this film, nearly two hundred million people have indicated decisions for Christ.[1]

On one occasion, the film was exhibited in a remote village in East Africa. The spectacle of a motion picture was miracle enough for these people—they had no idea such a phenomenon existed. And when the story of the life of Christ played out before their own eyes, in their own language and in living color, these dear people were captivated by what they beheld. To them it was as if the depicted scenes were taking place right there in the room. The people listened intently to the teachings of Jesus. They thrilled to the miracles. Then, chaos very nearly ensued.

The trial and physical beating of Jesus played out on the screen, and the viewers were enraged. They hurled weapons at the image and howled in protest. They stood and demanded that the beatings be halted!

The missionary briefly clicked off the projector and explained that the story was not yet over. So the people sat for the terrible crucifixion of our Lord. The grief in the room was overwhelming. The people wept and wailed so loudly that the projector was stopped again, and once again the missionary implored everyone to be patient for the ending.

Suddenly the blessed miracle of the resurrection occurred before the eyes of people who had no idea of what was coming.

The Best Friend they never knew had set them free, long ago and far away.

Uninhibited celebration broke out in that room—wild jubilation, dancing across overturned chairs, embraces and backslaps, helpless tears of sheer gratitude and wonder.[2]

This, my friend, is a picture of the reaction anyone would display if they lived under a death sentence, to suddenly be told that the sentence would be revoked, that the Best Friend they never knew had set them free, long ago and far away, and the news had just now arrived.

This is the delight you and I should feel about meeting Jesus, every morning and every moment. "A son is part of the family forever. So if the Son sets you free, you will indeed be free" (John 8:35–36). Life on this side of spiritual rebirth is an occasion for unbridled joy and celebration—and the beginning of the abundant life.

THE SECRET OF THE FIRST BELIEVERS

Why is it that we so seldom feel the overwhelming emotions of those new believers in East Africa? God has promised you, as a Christian, a legacy of support, abundance, and joy. Why, then, are so few Christians really enjoying their inheritance? Let me ask you: Are you living a joyous, fruitful life?

Based on the promises of Jesus, we should have joy enough to fill all of our days. Let us count our blessings:

We are free from the burden of sin (Revelation 1:5).

We are promised that we can do all things in Christ (Philippians 4:13).

We are promised that we can perform greater wonders than He himself accomplished in His earthly ministry (John 14:12).

We are promised that He will go with us, that He will empower us, and that His authority is ours (Matthew 28:18–20; Acts 1:8).

Why, then, our ho-hum attitudes toward life and our Lord?

In his introduction to *Letters to Young Churches*, J. B. Phillips wrote,

> The great difference between present-day Christianity and
> that of which we read in these letters [the New Testament
> epistles] is that to us it is primarily a performance; to them
> it was a real experience. We are apt to reduce the Christian
> religion to a code, or at best a rule of heart and life. To
> these men it is quite plainly the invasion of their lives by a

new quality of life altogether. They do not hesitate to describe this as Christ "living in" them ... Perhaps if we believed what they believed, we could achieve what they achieved.[3]

Phillips hit the nail on the head. The first-century church was so dynamic that it must have had a source outside this world. Filled with the Spirit and compelled by the love of God, the early church took the good news of God's love and forgiveness to every corner of the vast Roman Empire and beyond. Never before had any small body of ordinary men and women made such an impact on the world.

Those Christians were a group of ordinary people like you and me, but they truly knew the love and forgiveness of God. Controlled and empowered by God's Holy Spirit, they reached out in love to people living under the tyranny of an evil empire and ignited a spiritual revolution that would continue into eternity.

Even though we are surrounded by evil in this world, we are free from its power.

Had they relied upon their own personal resources, these early believers would have quickly faded into the dust of historical obscurity. They might better have picked up their fishing nets, returned to their plows, and gathered the pieces of their former lives. But Jesus was right—those men would indeed perform greater wonders. Where He had reached a handful, they reached across barriers of culture, geography, and language.

Were they extraordinary people? The truth is that those believers had no more talent or wisdom than you, and far fewer resources. Ordinary as they were, the early Christians truly knew the love and forgiveness of God.

And that very same power is available to you.

LIVING IN FREEDOM

Your very first step toward the abundant life is to realize your new relation toward sin. The nonbeliever must live a life of helpless submission to his or her sinful impulses. But you, as a follower of Christ, are free from that terrible tyrant of evil. Consider the full extent of your liberty:

- You have been freed from the *penalty* of sin. "There is no judgment awaiting those who trust him" (John 3:18).
- You are being freed from the *power* of sin. "And now, all glory to God, who is able to keep you from stumbling, and who will bring you into his glorious presence innocent of sin and with great joy" (Jude verse 24).
- And you will be freed from the very *presence* of sin. "But we do know that when he comes we will be like him" (1 John 3:2). One day our Lord "will transform our lowly bodies so that they will be like his glorious body" (Philippians 3:21 NIV).

Just as we accepted the gift of salvation by an act of faith, we must also accept the potential of the abundant life as an act of faith.

Isn't it exciting to know that, even though we are surrounded by evil in this world, we are free from its power? Still, this is a freedom we must *claim*. Just as we accepted the gift of salvation by an act of faith, we must also accept the potential of the abundant life as an act of faith. You can have millions of dollars in the bank, but you receive no benefit unless you draw from the account. In the same way, you must choose to live a life unencumbered by sin by confessing disobedience to God right away. Then it becomes possible to live the wonderful life of joy and abundance that Jesus wants us to have.

> So you should consider yourselves dead to sin and able to live for the glory of God through Christ Jesus.
>
> Do not let sin control the way you live; do not give in to its lustful desires. Do not let any part of your body become a tool of wickedness, to be used for sinning. Instead, give yourselves completely to God since you have been given new life. And use your whole body as a tool to do what is right for the glory of God. Sin is no longer your master, for you are no longer subject to the law, which enslaves you to sin. Instead, you are free by God's grace.
>
> ROMANS 6:11-14

COMMITMENT TO A NEW LIFE

Once you have freed yourself from the bondage of sinfulness, you commit yourself to a new way of living. "But now you are free from the power of sin and have become slaves of God. Now you do those things that lead to holiness and result in eternal life" (Romans 6:22). Your motives change. Your desires change. Your goals are now to achieve the results that bring pleasure to your Lord rather than your selfish appetites.

This kind of life is powerful and attractive. It is said that there was a Lutheran bishop imprisoned by the Nazis during the Second World War. His captors had to change the guards daily to keep them from being converted to the Christian faith!

That is the same power Paul had when he was imprisoned and the same overflowing appeal that enabled the first Christians to be so effective. Jesus said, "My purpose is to give life in all its fullness" (John 10:10). The original language carried the idea of an overflowing container. Not only is life full, but it seeps out the top so that whoever is around us cannot help but be refreshed. The early Christian Irenaeus said, "The glory of God is a human being fully alive."[4]

---❖---

Commit. Trust. Be still. Wait.

Therefore, commit yourself to God. Use Psalm 37 as your guide: "Commit everything you do to the LORD. Trust him, and he will help you. He will make your innocence as clear as the dawn, and the justice of your cause will shine like the noonday sun. Be still in the presence of the LORD, and wait patiently for him to act" (verses 5–7).

Take special notice of the verbs in that passage. These will become your action plan. The key ones are *commit*, *trust, be still*, and *wait*. Today, as you read this chapter, I recommend that you make those four action words the hallmark of your day. Let us consider what such a day will look like for you.

You begin with a sincere commitment of the day to God's glory. Meet with Him in the morning, when you and the day are both fresh and filled with potential. Spend time at His feet, in praise and worship of who He is. And make a covenant to return every hour and every moment He has given to you as a gift of devotion.

Continue by trusting Him to use you in a special way. By an act of faith, you simply acknowledge that He is going to be present and powerful in your life on this day. Already, even as you claim this promise, you will begin to feel the excitement.

Next, at all times, be still and wait patiently for Him to act. The key is to take the Lord with you as you rise to leave your private place of devotion. His Spirit is always present in your life, of course. You want to be more aware of His presence and sensitive to how He may be working in your life and the lives of others. You will see and discern truths that otherwise would have eluded you.

Last, wait patiently. Do not run ahead of Him, as Jonah did after he took God's message of warning to the Ninevites. Jonah was ready for God to destroy the city; He was not waiting on the Lord to make *His* will known. (See Jonah 3–4.) God always has His will and His time. Submit yourself to Him and wait in faith and expectancy.

REDESIGN YOUR LIFE

A rich man bought a special painting of Christ for his large and luxurious home. It was a lovely picture, and he could not decide exactly where to place it. So he called in a very wise interior designer who studied the various rooms of the home, then studied the picture with the same level of concentration. Finally he said, "Friend, the picture will not fit into your home."

The owner's face fell. "How could a picture of Jesus not fit here?" he asked. "He is my Lord and Savior—the center of all my being."

"I fully realize that," said the designer. "That is why you must design your entire home to fit this picture."

Yes, even as the temple of Jerusalem was constructed by Solomon—under God's design—to house the sacred law of

God, it is up to you now, beginning this very day, to redesign your life to correspond with the presence of Christ in you. This is not a task you can carry out in one day or in one week. Freed slaves continue to act in the pattern of slavery for a period of time until they become acquainted with the full range of their freedom. You have been a slave to sin, and now you need only the appropriate time and the loving, patient guidance of the Holy Spirit, who will direct you and mold you one day at a time, until you conform to the image of Christ himself.

Why would anyone want to delay something as wonderful as the abundant life?

But please begin today! Why would anyone want to delay something as wonderful as the abundant life, the overflowing life that brings such wonderful fruit?

> But when the Holy Spirit controls our lives, he will produce this kind of fruit in us: love, joy, peace, patience, kindness, goodness, faithfulness, gentleness, and self-control. Here there is no conflict with the law.
>
> Those who belong to Christ Jesus have nailed the passions and desires of their sinful nature to his cross and crucified them there. If we are living now by the Holy Spirit, let us follow the Holy Spirit's leading in every part of our lives.

GALATIANS 5:22–25

Today, as you spend time with God, make a list of the sins that need to be crucified. Write them down, and imagine yourself nailing them to the cross. As you do so, cross out each one.

———————❖———————

MEETING JESUS IS THE GREATEST MOMENT OF YOUR LIFE,
BUT KNOWING HIM IS THE ULTIMATE ADVENTURE.

———————————

Then thank your Lord that you can follow the Spirit from now on until all that wonderful and abundant fruit begins to blossom in the evergreen branches of your life. Joys unimaginable await you.

Let us consider how that blossoming—or growth—will take place.

---

1. Statistics taken from the *JESUS* Film Project Web site at http://www.jesusfilm.com/progress/statistics.html.

2. Ben Patterson, "Resurrection and Pandemonium," LeadershipJournal.net, 4/13/04.

3. J. B. Phillips, *Letters to Young Churches: A Translation of the New Testament Epistles* (New York: The Macmillan Company, 1948), p. xiv.

4. Jeff Imbach, "Whatever Happened to the Abundant Life?" *Discipleship Journal,* No. 107.

CHAPTER SIX

A Light for Every Path

———————❖———————

WHAT IS FAITH? IT IS THE CONFIDENT ASSURANCE THAT
WHAT WE HOPE FOR IS GOING TO HAPPEN. IT IS THE EVI-
DENCE OF THINGS WE CANNOT YET SEE.

HEBREWS 11:1

6

A Light for Every Path

Nathaniel Hawthorne wrote a fascinating short story called "The Great Stone Face." It concerned a country that lost its beloved king. So great was his popularity with the people that they determined not to replace him until they could find as perfect a replica as possible.

The people were serious about their intention. They even insisted that the future king must physically resemble the departed one. And to that end, they hired a gifted sculptor to carve the late king's profile into the side of a cliff. This way, his face would be ever before the people as they waited for fate to deliver into their hands his successor.

A grand commission traveled the countryside for years in search of the right man, but they could never find him. Years passed into generations, and still there was no successor to the king. But through the many decades, the country kept up its search, even as its glory faded for lack of leadership. The men traveled and they searched, but they were now long past expecting that they would ever find the man to match the carving.

Then one day they came to a little peasant cottage, nestled just beneath the great rocky profile of the ancient king. The searchers were shocked: Here, finally, was the man! The cliff was right before them, and a young man stood beneath it—the very image of that classic profile.

As a child that young man had been thrilled to hear the legend of the Great Stone Face from his mother. He became caught up in the hope of recognizing that long-expected leader when he finally came. And so he intently studied the face in the cliff every single day. He memorized every feature, even the subtle flaws in the carving—until, after years of scrutiny, he had come to bear the image himself, without even realizing it. And the country had a new king.

> *Meeting Jesus is the greatest moment of your life, but knowing Him is the ultimate adventure.*

Meeting Jesus is the greatest moment of your life, but knowing Him is the ultimate adventure. The wonderful thing about our faith is that friendship with our Lord grows sweeter and stronger every day. Many people fear aging, but those who know Jesus simply look forward to growing still further into His image. Like the boy meditating upon the Great Stone Face, we eventually come to resemble the Christ we adore.

How often have we heard this very truism in the example of older married couples? It is said that after many years of marriage, a husband and wife will come to resemble one another! We laugh about the idea, but there is a genuine principle here. What we truly value determines what we become. When Moses came down from the mountain where he beheld God's glory, he wore a veil so people would not be blinded by God's light reflecting from his face. In 2 Corinthians 3:18, Paul makes the point that those who do not know God are veiled and blinded from the truth. But "all of us have had that veil removed so that we can be mirrors that brightly reflect the glory of the Lord. And as the Spirit of the Lord works within us, we become more and more like him and reflect his glory even more."

What a great thought! The glory of God on the face of Moses faded, but in your case it will be the old sinful countenance that will fade, because you can experience His glory every day and become more and more like Him.

You will have set out on the grand expedition of daily growth—a journey of transformation. This is the key to becoming more like Christ: daily growth—not transient feelings.

Let us take a moment to examine this important idea a bit closer.

STAYING ON TRACK

Picture for yourself an old-fashioned, coal-burning train. The train illustrates the relationship between fact (God and His Word), faith (our trust in God and His Word), and feelings (the result of our faith and obedience).

Fact is the locomotive.

Faith is the coal car, which provides fuel for the locomotive.

And *feeling* is the caboose. The train will run with or without the caboose. However, it would be futile to attempt to pull the train by the caboose. In the same way, we as Christians do not depend on feelings or emotions, though they have their place in our experience. We place our faith in the trustworthiness of God and the promises of His Word.

Your faith is propelled down the tracks of life by the absolute, empirical fact of Christ in this world, slain for our sins, and risen to defeat death and open the way for us to live a new and eternal life. Our faith follows along, and wonderful, joyful emotions inevitably come, too. But our faith is based on the facts that lead, rather than the feelings that follow.

—————❖—————

Spiritual growth results from trusting Jesus Christ as Lord, Savior, Master, and King.

Therefore, when you experience those dry days, when your enthusiasm wanes just a bit, please do not conclude that something is wrong with your faith. Feelings come and go, but facts are concrete and unchangeable.

Now that you've entered into a personal relationship with Christ, many exciting and wonderful things have happened to you. Let us review them.

1. Christ came into your life.
2. Your sins were forgiven.
3. You became a child of God.
4. You received eternal life.
5. You began the great adventure for which God created you.

Can you think of anything more wonderful? Why not pause right now and thank God in prayer for what He has done for you? By thanking God, you demonstrate your faith. You may want to pray something like this:

Dear Lord, Thank You for coming into my life. Thank You for forgiving all the wrong things that I've done and for making me Your child. Thank You that I will spend eternity with You and that I can begin right now to live the life You designed me to live. Live out Your life through me, Lord. In the wonderful name of Jesus, amen.

Spiritual growth results from trusting Jesus Christ as Lord, Savior, Master, and King. The more you put your trust in Him, the freer you will become. The key to the rest of your life will be the ongoing lesson of learning to live by faith rather than sight. Galatians 3:11 (NASB) tells us, "The righteous man shall live by faith."

GROWING STRONGER

The daily stretching of your faith, like developing a muscle, will make you stronger and stronger in the faith. A life of faith will enable you to increasingly trust God with every detail of your life. Just as a young athlete might use several different kinds of exercises and workout routines to condition his or her body, you will use six different spiritual disciplines to build your faith. In order to help you remember them daily, we have worked out an acrostic, "GROWTH," to help you keep them in mind.

G*o to God in Prayer Daily*

Seven days make one week, but it has also been observed that seven days without prayer makes one *weak*. There is no stationary position in the Christian life; we are either moving closer to our Lord or further away every day. You need to practice daily prayer, praising Him, abiding in Him, and taking every burden and care to Him. Paul writes, "Don't worry about anything; instead, pray about everything. Tell God what you need, and thank him for all he has done. If you do this, you will experience God's peace, which is far more wonderful than the human mind can understand. His peace will guard your hearts and minds as you live in Christ Jesus" (Philippians 4:6–7).

A friend of mine plugs a pocket-sized, handheld computer into his desktop computer through a cable. Agendas, notes, calendar items, and new contacts flow to the handheld machine from the larger one—and the pocket computer sends all its new information to the desktop. The smaller one then becomes a "portable" version of the larger computer.

Prayer is the "cable" by which we connect with our Lord each day to stay synchronized with Him, to keep our agenda based on God so that we may become smaller versions of Christ in this world. We must abide in Christ, or we will become spiritually dry. Jesus said, "Remain in me, and I will remain in you. For a branch cannot produce fruit if it is severed from the vine, and you cannot be fruitful apart from me" (John 15:4).

*R*ead God's Word Daily

Prayer and God's Word go hand in hand. Our hearts connect with God through prayer, while our minds grow in faith through Bible study. You will spend a lifetime studying the Scriptures and never exhaust their riches, for each time you read, the Holy Spirit will apply the words and thoughts to your experience.

I have recommended starting with the gospel of John. You will also want to read some of the letters, such as 1 John and Paul's letter to the Philippians. And soon, you will want to read all the way through God's Word. There are many good plans for reading through the Word in one year; ask your pastor or a Christian friend to help you find one. What a wonderful adventure you will have in devoting yourself to all the great treasures in Scripture: the key themes, the unforgettable characters, the wonderful stories, and the realization that all of Scripture comes from the very heart of God. Paul tells us, "All Scripture is inspired by God and is useful to teach us what is true and to make us realize what is wrong in our lives. It straightens us out and teaches us to do what is right. It is God's way of preparing us in every way, fully equipped for every good thing God wants us to do" (2 Timothy 3:16–17).

> ❖
>
> *Jesus is saying that a sure way to grow is to simply obey Him.*

Obey God Moment by Moment

Obedience is the ultimate test of our faith. Each of us will stumble occasionally, but a child of God is marked by consistent obedience to Christ and His Word. "All who believe in God's Son have eternal life. Those who don't obey the Son will never experience eternal life, but the wrath of God remains upon them" (John 3:36). In other words, persistent disobedience is the sign that someone has not trusted Christ as Lord and Savior.

Jesus stated it simply: "Those who obey my commandments are the ones who love me. And because they love me, my Father will love them, and I will love them. And I will reveal myself to each one of them" (John 14:21). Jesus is saying that a sure way to grow is to simply obey Him, for the more you carry out His will, the more you will know Him; and the more you know Him, the more you will grow.

But how will you know what He wants? Pray daily and remain in the Word; all six of these "GROWTH" exercises supplement each other. The Spirit will instruct your heart, and the

Word will instruct your mind. Obedience is putting those instructions into physical action.

Witness for Christ by Your Life and Words

The greatest privilege we have in life is to share our faith with others who do not know Christ. The first command Jesus ever gave His disciples was, "Follow Me, and I will make you fishers of men" (Matthew 4:19 NKJV). The last command was a restatement of His mission statement and ours: "Therefore, go and make disciples of all the nations, baptizing them in the name of the Father and the Son and the Holy Spirit. Teach these new disciples to obey all the commands I have given you. And be sure of this: I am with you always, even to the end of the age" (Matthew 28:19–20).

Some have estimated that no more than one believer in twenty has experienced the unique joy of leading another soul to Christ. This is a tragic fact not simply for those who need to hear, but for those who need to tell. After many decades of sharing my faith, I can testify that nothing brings me greater pleasure and deeper satisfaction than on those occasions when the Holy Spirit uses my life and my willingness to help some other soul accept the wonderful gift of salvation.

David Brainerd, the missionary, spent his short life sharing the gospel with Indians on the banks of the Delaware. He said, "I care not where I live, or what hardships I go through, so that I can but gain souls to Christ. While I am asleep, I dream of these things; as soon as I awake, the first thing I think of is this great work. All my desire is the conversion of sinners, and all my hope is in God."[1]

I always ask my Christian friends, "What is the greatest thing you could do for another person?" The answer is clear.

But so many people are too timid to share their faith. They fail to grasp the fact that God's Spirit will use us in every situation; He will give us the boldness, the opportunities, and the words. All we need to do is present our Lord a willing spirit. God has performed some of the mightiest feats in human history through timid but willing vessels.

*T*rust God for Every Detail of Your Life

"What is faith? It is the confident assurance that what we hope for is going to happen. It is the evidence of things we cannot yet see" (Hebrews 11:1). One factor that sets us, as believers, apart from the world is our absolute trust in God. The world walks by sight, but we walk by faith. We know that our God is in control not simply of the great world events, but of the details of life. And we refuse to worry about

> *God has performed some of the mightiest feats in human history through timid but willing vessels.*

these details because we know our Lord will care for us. During His Sermon on the Mount, Jesus commanded us to trust Him completely for all the needs of life: "So I tell you, don't worry about everyday life—whether you have enough food, drink, and clothes. Doesn't life consist of more than food and clothing? Look at the birds. They don't need to plant or harvest or put food in barns because your heavenly Father feeds them. And you are far more valuable to him than they are. Can all your worries add a single moment to your life? Of course not" (Matthew 6:25–27).

And as Paul has taught us, "Don't worry about anything; instead, pray about everything. Tell God what you need, and thank him for all he has done. If you do this, you will experience

God's peace, which is far more wonderful than the human mind can understand. His peace will guard your hearts and minds as you live in Christ Jesus" (Philippians 4:6–7).

Being a Christian does not mean freedom from problems. But it does mean we need not carry the burden of those problems. We trust them to our Lord and enjoy His wonderful peace.

Allow the *H*oly Spirit to Control You

When you became a Christian, God's Holy Spirit came to live within you. As a matter of fact, on the eve of His trial, Jesus told His disciples that it was better that He leave, so that the Holy Spirit could come. He told them to wait and do nothing until that Spirit came: "But when the Holy Spirit has come upon you, you will receive power and will tell people about me everywhere—in Jerusalem, throughout Judea, in Samaria, and to the ends of the earth" (Acts 1:8).

In other words, we can accomplish nothing in our own power. Without His indwelling us, we would be no different from any unbeliever. But when the Spirit indwells your heart, it is even better than having Christ in your presence, as the disciples had—because He is actually *within* you, providing more ministries than we can take the time to relate in these brief pages. He guides you and teaches you. He gently convicts you of sin. He comforts you. He gives you your special spiritual gifts to allow you to function helpfully among other believers. He even helps you pray when you lack the knowledge of what to pray for. "If we are living now by the Holy Spirit, let us follow the Holy Spirit's leading in every part of our lives" (Galatians 5:25).

Also, find a good church to attend where you can grow and

have fellowship with other believers in Christ. In Hebrews 10:25, God's Word admonishes us not to forsake the assembling of ourselves together. You see, several logs burn brightly together, but putting one log aside on the cold hearth makes the fire goes out. So it is with your relationship with other Christians.

If you do not belong to a church, do not wait to be invited. Take the initiative! Call the pastor of a nearby church where Christ is honored and the Word of God is preached. Start this week and make plans to attend regularly.

God bless you! Welcome to the family of God, and welcome to a rewarding life of intimacy with our creator God and Savior and the great adventure of fulfilling His plan for your life.

I have walked with Jesus for more than five decades, and I can tell you that He loves you. He has a wonderful plan for you. All you have to do is love, trust, and obey Him, and you will embark on an exciting adventure.

God bless you as you discover how Jesus will meet your every need—until that day when we meet Him face-to-face. In our next chapter, we will have a foretaste of that future glory!

---

1. Paul Lee Tan, *Encyclopedia of 7,700 Illustrations* (Rockville, MD: Assurance Publishers), Bible Communications Inc.

—————❖—————

You and I can eagerly await that time
when we shall find rest and when Jesus will
wipe away every tear. But in the meantime,
we have a world to serve.

—————————

CHAPTER SEVEN

A King for All Eternity

---❖---

Now we see things imperfectly as in a poor mirror, but then we will see everything with perfect clarity. All that I know now is partial and incomplete, but then I will know everything completely, just as God knows me now.

1 Corinthians 13:12

7

A King for All Eternity

Alittle boy stood with his parents at a high point among the Rocky Mountains. The air was thin and cool. The peaks rose majestically in every direction, covered with a soft blanket of snow as they climbed into the winter sky.

The family stood quietly, taking in the awesome beauty of the view, listening to the stillness of the silence, and watching their breath turn to mist. After a few moments, the father asked his son what he thought of the mountains. The little boy said, "If this side of heaven is so wonderful, what must the other side look like?"

Sometimes it takes the simple grasp of a child to capture the deeper truths. Indeed, how lovely must heaven be? This world, fallen though it is, glistens with the marvelous ingenuity and pervasive poetry of the Creator Artist who rendered everything from the simplest atom to the most distant galaxy. The fantastic vistas of this world are enough to convince our limited human minds of the greatness of God. Yet we know that the deepest pleasures of this life, the most profound delights of godly living, and the most satisfying human relationships we can enjoy will all seem miniscule in comparison to the joys that await us.

After you have met Jesus, your life will be radically transformed for many reasons. The Holy Spirit will guide you toward a new life that pleases your Lord. But you will also live with the hope of eternity ever before you: the goal of one day meeting Jesus face-to-face. The Bible assures us that this is an eventuality. At the time when His earthly ministry was drawing

> *After you have met Jesus, your life will be radically transformed.*

to a close, Jesus gave us His promise that one of His purposes between then and now would be to prepare an eternal home for us. He said, "There are many rooms in my Father's home, and I am going to prepare a place for you. If this were not so, I would tell you plainly. When everything is ready, I will come and get you, so that you will always be with me where I am. And you know where I am going and how to get there" (John 14:2–4).

Take a moment to picture the perfect heavenly home lovingly prepared for us by our Savior and Lord. Of course, no matter how much we might cherish such a picture, it defies human imagination. Our minds cannot hold the power and magnitude of something so transcendently wonderful.

THE EXPECTANCY OF HEAVEN

But living in expectancy of heaven is like living all of life in the manner of a small child waiting for the delights of Christmas morning. Such a child has extra energy and joy, shining eyes, future focus. As believers in heaven, we know that eternity will be wonderful beyond imagining—and unlike

Christmas morning, the joy will not end. The decorations will not fade. The music will not cease.

For you and me, the certain hope of that world should transform the reality of this one.

There was once a great old preacher named John Jasper. He was a onetime slave who was set free after the War between the States. He was a delightful, joyous believer who served as pastor of a church called the Sixth Mt. Zion Baptist Church in Richmond, Virginia.

One day John Jasper was preaching on the inexpressible joys of heaven. He wanted to paint a picture in words of the glories that awaited his congregation. But as he stood in the pulpit and his heart, mind, and soul became caught up in the wonderful subject, he found that no words would come. He was rendered speechless. Can you imagine such a plight for a preacher whose art was word craft?

The congregation sat patiently and waited, but the pastor could not extract a single sentence through the constraints of his emotion. Tears welled up in his eyes, and they began to roll down his cheeks. Finally he lifted his hands to his people in a dismissive wave toward the exits. There would be no more sermon today—yet no one moved. The pastor had his hand on the door himself, but he saw that his people still sat in expectancy.

He managed to walk back to the pulpit, his hands shaking, and say, "Brothers and sisters, when I think of the glory which shall be revealed in us, I can visualize that day when old John Jasper's last battle has been fought and the last burden has been borne. I can visualize that day when this tired servant of God shall lay down his burdens and walk up to the battlements of the City of God. Then as I stand outside the beautiful gate,

I can almost hear the Mighty Angel on guard say, 'John Jasper, you want your shoes?'

"And I reply, 'Of course I want those golden slippers, but not now.'

"Then," he continued, "I can hear the Mighty Angel as he says, 'John Jasper, don't you want your robe?'"

"And I'd say, 'Of course I want that fine robe of righteousness, but not now.'

The preacher continued in this vein, imagining every heavenly reward that could be offered to him—along with the chance to meet Elijah, who called down fire from heaven; with David; with Moses; and with Paul himself, the greatest soul winner in the Bible. But John Jasper intended to politely decline each of those offers, saying, "I want to shake the hand of each of them and to be reunited with many of my loved ones who have waited for me here. But not now. Not until later, if it's all the same to you. First of all, I want only to see *Jesus*."

Crowns and mansions will be splendid. Being in the company of the saints will be a joy beyond all comprehension. But nothing can compare to the prospect of seeing Jesus face-to-face. Have you ever stopped to fully consider that you will stand before Him someday? As Paul has written, "Now we see things imperfectly as in a poor mirror, but then we will see everything with perfect clarity. All that I know now is partial and incomplete, but then I will know everything completely, just as God knows me now" (1 Corinthians 13:12).

I long for that day, as I am certain you do—the chance to have every question answered, the chance to have every tear wiped away, the chance to see all pain and death and evil destroyed forever. But even through the "poor mirror" of this world, of our limited minds, of this book, of every possible attempt to understand, we nonetheless *do* comprehend that the greatest joy of all will be coming into the very presence of our Lord and Savior, and knowing that we have all of eternity to spend in His perfect, righteous, loving presence. Meeting Jesus now is heavenly, but heaven itself will be *meeting Jesus* face-to-face.

MEANWHILE ...

Only one human being has beheld heaven and brought back a report. John, the Beloved Disciple, was given a preview to serve as encouragement during times of persecution and to stand forever as the closing movement of the Word of God. We find John's report in the book of Revelation, where he tells us, "And I heard a voice from heaven saying, 'Write this down: Blessed are those who die in the Lord from now on. Yes, says the Spirit, they are blessed indeed, for they will rest from all their toils and trials; for their good deeds follow them!'" (Revelation 14:13).

You and I can eagerly await that time when we shall find rest and when Jesus will wipe away every tear. But in the meantime, we have a world to serve. Jesus sent a message through the Holy Spirit that our good deeds will follow us to paradise.

Meeting Jesus now is heavenly, but heaven itself will be meeting Jesus face-to-face.

I HAVE FOUGHT A GOOD FIGHT, I HAVE FINISHED THE RACE, AND I HAVE REMAINED FAITHFUL. AND NOW THE PRIZE AWAITS ME ... AND THE PRIZE IS NOT JUST FOR ME BUT FOR ALL WHO EAGERLY LOOK FORWARD TO HIS GLORIOUS RETURN.

2 TIMOTHY 4:7–8

CHAPTER EIGHT

Live It!

---◆---

AS I HAVE SERVED HIM THROUGH THESE MANY
DECADES, I CAN ASSURE YOU THAT EVERY DAY WITH
JESUS IS SWEETER THAN THE DAY BEFORE.

8

Live It!

Hebrews 11 reviews many of the great personal stories of the Old Testament—from Abraham to Joseph, from Moses to David. The message is that God's people were driven to great achievement by the thought of the heaven that was now invisible, but surely awaited them:

> Abraham did this because he was confidently looking
> forward to a city with eternal foundations, a city designed
> and built by God ... All these faithful ones died without
> receiving what God had promised them, but they saw it all
> from a distance and welcomed the promises of God. They
> agreed that they were no more than foreigners and nomads
> here on earth. And obviously people who talk like that are
> looking forward to a country they can call their own. If
> they had meant the country they came from, they would
> have found a way to go back. But they were looking for a
> better place, a heavenly homeland. That is why God is not

ashamed to be called their God, for he has prepared a heavenly city for them.

HEBREWS 11:10, 13–16

These were people always looking forward, always on the move—nomads searching for the eternity they knew to be their rightful home. They kept their eyes on the prize. The passage concludes that we "can't receive the prize at the end of the race until we finish the race" (verse 40).

In summary, life is a race—a preliminary event in the Eternal Olympics. Like God's champions from Hebrews 11, we run with the thought of a future prize. We are ambassadors from another world (see 2 Corinthians 5:20), awaiting our true fulfillment when we finally return home to our awaiting Father. We reject the world's standards for those of Christ because we have faith that the prize awaits us when we finish the race.

This does not mean, of course, that we regard this world and its needs as unimportant. We know that God has placed us in this world for reasons that impact the next one. In short, the Lord wants us to walk in faith toward the ultimate destination and gather as many other travelers as possible to make the journey with us. Whenever you lead a friend to Christ, you have done something miraculous and wonderful: You have enlarged the very borders of heaven.

What does this mean? We live with our feet squarely in this world and our hearts in the next. We give all of our energy to serving God right now, knowing that our ultimate destination is the very presence of God. We want to stand before Him someday and receive the crown that is offered to those who served Him well. The attitude we want to have is best exemplified by Paul, who wrote, "I have fought a good fight, I have finished the race, and I have remained faithful. And now the prize awaits me—the crown of righteousness that the Lord, the righteous Judge, will give me on that great day of his return. And the prize is not just for me but for all who eagerly look forward to his glorious return" (2 Timothy 4:7–8).

You may have heard it said of certain people that they are "so heavenly minded that they are of no earthly good." Please avoid becoming that kind of person! Paul was as heavenly minded as we can imagine, yet he succeeded in assembling through his life a

Consider the end of this book to be the beginning of true life for you.

small army of converts to make the trip to heaven. The Great Commandment requires you to love the Lord your God with all your heart, soul, mind, and strength and to love your neighbor as you would love yourself (see Matthew 22:37–40). Serving God and others will keep you busy in this life, and it will be the perfect preparation for your new home someday.

And therefore consider the end of this book to be the beginning of true life for you. I urge you to continue in good works for the kingdom of God. Meet Jesus daily through prayer and study of the Word. Meet Him through serving your fellow believers and sharing your faith with those who do not know the Lord. Meet Jesus through living and loving by faith every step of the way, no matter what the world may say and do.

I hope and, more, I pray that you have already met Jesus in a new way through these chapters we have shared. But meeting Him is not a onetime event; it is a lifetime adventure that grows deeper, more powerful, and more fruitful every day.

As I have served Him through these many decades, I can assure you that every day with Jesus is sweeter than the day before.

Yes, it is true that the Bible tells us that "Jesus Christ is the same yesterday, today, and forever" (Hebrews 13:8). He does not change—but *you* will. Since you first opened the front cover of this book, you have changed. With every chapter, with every initiative in coming to know Jesus better, you have taken part in the process of transformation. The Spirit has begun a good work in your life, my friend, and He will carry it forward to completion, from your meeting with Jesus today, until that eternal sunset when you will stand before Him, lay all your treasures at His feet, and hear Him say the words every believer longs to hear: "Well done, my good and faithful servant" (Matthew 25:21).

A Prayer and a Promise

It would be highly appropriate for you and me to close this book together with a prayer and a promise. First, I urge you to make a covenant before Christ that you will begin today to come to know Him as well as He can be known in this life; that you will serve Him with all your strength; that you will testify to Him among all those people who come across your path; that you will serve Him as Lord unconditionally from now until eternity. Write down your promise in your own words. Do so in a private place, and then make it your prayer. Read it aloud before your own ears and before the Lord himself. Keep a small copy of this covenant with you wherever you go, and rededicate yourself to the Lord's service daily.

You might offer a daily prayer to God that goes something like this:

Blessed Lord Jesus, how wonderful, how majestic is Your name. I have begun the adventure of coming to know You, and I realize that this is the greatest gift that life offers. I know that You are preparing a place for me in heaven. I know that You want me to live the abundant life on this earth—a life of joy and service. I know that You want me to grow daily by abiding in You and that You will lead me to share my faith with nonbelievers. What a wonderful life is ahead for me, dedicating every day and every moment and every breath to Your service! Go with me now, as I know You will, as I serve as Your ambassador to this needy world. May You and I meet daily and be inseparable for all of this life, until the day when we finally meet face-to-face. In Your blessed and powerful name, amen.

Readers' Guide

FOR PERSONAL REFLECTION
OR GROUP DISCUSSION

Questions are an inevitable part of life. Proud parents ask their new baby, "Can you smile?" Later they ask, "Can you say 'Mama'?" "Can you walk to Daddy?" The early school years bring the inevitable, "What did you learn at school today?" Later school years introduce tougher questions, "If X equals 12 and Y equals –14, then …?" Adulthood adds a whole new set of questions. "Should I remain single or marry?" "How did things go at the office?" "Did you get a raise?" "Should we let Susie start dating?" "Which college is right for Kyle?" "How can we possibly afford to send our kids to college?"

This book raises questions, too. The following study guide is designed to (1) maximize the subject material and (2) apply biblical truth to daily life. You won't be asked to solve any algebraic problems or recall dates associated with obscure events in history, so relax. Questions asking for objective information are based solely on the text. Most questions, however, prompt you to search inside your soul, examine the circumstances that surround your life, and decide how you can best use the truths communicated in the book.

Honest answers to real issues can strengthen your faith, draw you closer to the Lord, and lead you into fuller, richer, more joyful, and productive daily adventures. So confront each question head-on and expect the One who is the answer for all of life's questions and needs to accomplish great things in your life.

CHAPTER 1: THE MAN WHO CHANGED HISTORY

1. How has Jesus left an indelible mark on history?

2. How has Jesus Christ changed the life of someone you know well?

3. Do you agree or disagree that anyone who follows human logic must conclude that Jesus is the Son of God? Defend your answer.

4. How does faith in Jesus Christ differ from religion?

5. How does the truth of the resurrection impact your life?

CHAPTER 2: A FRIEND FOR EVERY SEASON

1. How did Jesus show the Father's love for us?

2. The four gospels present a portrait of Jesus, each in a different light. Describe each.

3. How would you answer someone who claims Jesus was not the Son of God?

4. Read Hebrews 13:8. How does this verse encourage you to rely on Jesus' help today?

5. What does calling Jesus "Lord" mean in terms of daily living?

CHAPTER 3: A GIFT FOR EVERY NEED

1. What basic needs of the soul are universal?

2. In what ways do people everywhere show a restlessness that only Jesus can satisfy?

3. What longing for unconditional love and acceptance have you witnessed?

4. How is God able to offer individuals unconditional love and acceptance?

5. Why do you agree or disagree that lasting security and genuine significance are found only in a relationship with Jesus Christ?

CHAPTER 4: A DECISION FOR EVERY LIFE

1. Why do you agree or disagree that God's love for sinners is unmerited and inexplicable?

2. Why did God create the human race?

3. What does "death" mean in Romans 6:23?

4. What do you consider the worst aspect of eternal judgment? Explain your reason.

5. How would you explain the way of salvation to a seeker?

CHAPTER 5: A PURPOSE FOR EVERY MOMENT

1. In what ways is the Christian life "an exciting, abundant adventure"?

2. How do you explain the fact that many Christians fail to pursue this kind of adventure?

3. How well does the twenty-first-century church measure up to the first-century church in terms of joy and excitement about the task of sharing the good news? Defend your answer.

4. What is the first step toward the abundant life?

5. How will you rearrange your life to honor Jesus as Lord?

CHAPTER 6: A LIGHT FOR EVERY PATH

1. If you compared the Christian life to a thousand-mile journey, where would you mark your coming to know Christ as Savior? Which mile marker have you reached today? Are you pleased with your progress? Why or why not?

2. What spiritual goals do you wish to reach this year? Five years from now?

3. How can Christians put discouragement behind them?

4. What six spiritual disciplines associated with the acrostic "GROWTH" strengthen our faith?

5. What has God done in the past that encourages you to trust Him in the future?

CHAPTER 7: A KING FOR ALL ETERNITY

1. How does the hope of heaven impact the way Christians live today?

2. What features of heaven attract you most to your eternal home?

3. What is transpiring on earth today that will not take place in heaven?

4. If you have an opportunity to say a few words to Jesus when you meet Him in heaven, what will you say?

5. Why has Jesus left Christians on earth?

CHAPTER 8: LIVE IT!

1. How do you define "faith"?

2. What differences, if any, do you see between faith and hope?

3. Do you consider the Christian race a sprint or a marathon? Explain.

4. In what sense are some Christians so "heaven" minded that they are of no earthly good?

5. If a fellow believer asked you how to make every day with Jesus sweeter than the day before, what would say?

Appendix A

Would You Like to Know God Personally?

The following four principles will help you discover how to know God personally and experience the abundant life He promised.

God **loves** you and created you to know Him personally.

(References contained in this booklet should be read in context from the Bible wherever possible.)

God's Love

"God so loved the world, that He gave His only begotten Son, that whoever believes in Him should not perish, but have eternal life" (John 3:16).

God's Plan

"Now this is eternal life: that they may know you, the only true God, and Jesus Christ, whom you have sent" (John 17:3, NIV).

What prevents us from knowing God personally?

Man is **sinful** and **separated** from God, so we cannot know Him personally or experience His love.

Man Is Sinful

"All have sinned and fall short of the glory of God" (Romans 3:23).

Man was created to have fellowship with God; but, because of his own stubborn self-will, he chose to go his own independent way and fellowship with God was broken. This self-will, characterized by an attitude of active rebellion or passive indifference, is an evidence of what the Bible calls sin.

Man Is Separated

"The wages of sin is death" [spiritual separation from God] (Romans 6:23).

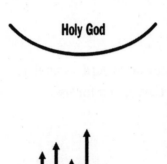

This diagram illustrates that God is holy and man is sinful. A great gulf separates the two. The arrows illustrate that man is continually trying to reach God and establish a personal relationship with Him through his own efforts, such as a good life, philosophy, or religion—but he inevitably fails.

The third principle explains the only way to bridge this gulf...

 Jesus Christ is God's **only** provision for man's sin. Through Him alone we can know God personally and experience God's love.

He Died In Our Place

"God demonstrates His own love toward us, in that while we were yet sinners, Christ died for us" (Romans 5:8).

He Rose From the Dead

"Christ died for our sins… He was buried… He was raised on the third day according to the Scriptures… He appeared to Peter, then to the twelve. After that He appeared to more than five hundred…" (1 Corinthians 15:3–6).

He Is the Only Way to God

"Jesus said to him, 'I am the way, and the truth, and the life; no one comes to the Father, but through Me'" (John 14:6).

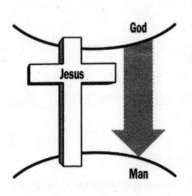

This diagram illustrates that God has bridged the gulf that separates us from Him by sending His Son, Jesus Christ, to die on the cross in our place to pay the penalty for our sins.

It is not enough just to know these truths...

 We must individually **receive** Jesus Christ as Savior and Lord; then we can know God personally and experience His love.

■ ■ ■ ■ ■ ■ ■ ■

We Must Receive Christ

"As many as received Him, to them He gave the right to become children of God, even to those who believe in His name" (John 1:12).

We Receive Christ Through Faith

"By grace you have been saved through faith; and that not of yourselves, it is the gift of God; not as a result of works that no one should boast" (Ephesians 2:8,9).

When We Receive Christ, We Experience a New Birth

(Read John 3:1–8.)

———

We Receive Christ By Personal Invitation

[Christ speaking] "Behold, I stand at the door and knock; if anyone hears My voice and opens the door, I will come in to him" (Revelation 3:20).

Receiving Christ involves turning to God from self (repentance) and trusting Christ to come into our lives to forgive us of our sins and to make us what He wants us to be. Just to agree intellectually that Jesus Christ is the Son of God and that He died on the cross for our sins is not enough. Nor is it enough to have an emotional experience. We receive Jesus Christ by faith, as an act of our will.

These two circles represent two kinds of lives:

Self-Directed Life

S – Self is on the throne

† – Christ is outside the life

● – Interests are directed by self, often resulting in discord and frustration

Christ-Directed Life

† – Christ is in the life and on the throne

S – Self is yielding to Christ

● – Interests are directed by Christ, resulting in harmony with God's plan

Which circle best represents your life?

Which circle would you like to have represent your life?

The following explains how you can receive Christ:

You Can Receive Christ Right Now
By Faith Through Prayer
(Prayer is talking with God)

God knows your heart and is not so concerned with your words as He is with the attitude of your heart. The following is a suggested prayer:

> *Lord Jesus, I want to know You personally. Thank You for dying on the cross for my sins. I open the door of my life and receive You as my Savior and Lord. Thank You for forgiving me of my sins and giving me eternal life. Take control of the throne of my life. Make me the kind of person You want me to be.*

Does this prayer express the desire of your heart?

If it does, pray this prayer right now, and Christ will come into your life, as He promised.

How to Know That Christ Is in Your Life

Did you receive Christ into your life? According to His promise in Revelation 3:20, where is Christ right now in relation to you? Christ said that He would come into your life and be your friend so you can know Him personally. Would He mislead you? On what authority do you know that God has answered your prayer? (The trustworthiness of God Himself and His Word.)

The Bible Promises Eternal Life to All Who Receive Christ

"The witness is this, that God has given us eternal life, and this life is in His Son. He who has the Son has the life; he who does not have the Son of God does not have the life. These things I have written to you who believe in the name of the Son of God, in order that you may know that you have eternal life" (1 John 5:11–13).

Thank God often that Christ is in your life and that He will never leave you (Hebrews 13:5). You can know on the basis of His promise that Christ lives in you and that you have eternal life from the very moment you invite Him in. He will not deceive you.

An important reminder...

Do Not Depend on Feelings

The promise of God's Word, the Bible—not our feelings—is our authority. The Christian lives by faith (trust) in the trustworthiness of God Himself and His Word. This train diagram illustrates the relationship among fact (God and His Word), faith (our trust in God and His Word), and feeling (the result of our faith and obedience) (John 14:21).

The train will run with or without the caboose. However, it would be useless to attempt to pull the train by the caboose. In the same way, we as Christians do not depend on feelings or emotions, but we place our faith (trust) in the trustworthiness of God and the promises of His Word.

Now That You Have Entered Into a Personal Relationship With Christ

The moment you received Christ by faith, as an act of your will, many things happened, including the following:

1. Christ came into your life (Revelation 3:20 and Colossians 1:27).

2. Your sins were forgiven (Colossians 1:14).

3. You became a child of God (John 1:12).

4. You received eternal life (John 5:24).

5. You began the great adventure for which God created you (John 10:10; 2 Corinthians 5:17; and 1 Thessalonians 5:18).

Can you think of anything more wonderful that could happen to you than entering into a personal relationship with Jesus Christ? Would you like to thank God in prayer right now for what He has done for you? By thanking God, you demonstrate your faith.

To enjoy your new relationship with God...

Suggestions for Christian Growth

Spiritual growth results from trusting Jesus Christ. "The righteous man shall live by faith" (Galatians 3:11). A life of faith will enable you to trust God increasingly with every detail of your life, and to practice the following:

G Go to God in prayer daily (John 15:7).

R Read God's Word daily (Acts 17:11)—begin with the Gospel of John.

O Obey God moment by moment (John 14:21).

W Witness for Christ by your life and words (Matthew 4:19; John 15:8).

T Trust God for every detail of your life (1 Peter 5:7).

H Holy Spirit—Allow Him to control and empower your daily life and witness (Galatians 5:16,17; Acts 1:8).

Appendix B

God's Word on Finding Jesus

Following are selected Scripture references that were presented throughout the text of this book. We encourage you to sit down with your Bible and review these verses in their context, prayerfully reflecting upon what God's Word tells you about the joy of finding Jesus.

CHAPTER 1

John 10:30

John 14:9

Acts 17:11–12

John 8:25

Colossians 1:15–16

Ephesians 1:9–10

Philippians 1:21

Psalm 34:8

Psalm 37:4–5

CHAPTER 2

Jeremiah 31:3

John 14:6–7

Philippians 2:6–7

Matthew 19:14

Matthew 9:36

Mark 1:40–44

1 John 4:8, 16

John 15:13–15

Mark 1:35

Matthew 26:39

Mark 4:41

John 11

Luke 7:11–17

Luke 8:49–56

John 19:10–11

Philippians 2:8–11

Matthew 22:37–38

CHAPTER 3

Romans 8:31–35, 37–39

Luke 12:16–21

Proverbs 3:25–26

Isaiah 41:10

Matthew 7:24–25

1 Corinthians 3:11–15

Matthew 6:33
John 14:17

CHAPTER 4

Revelation 3:20
John 3:16
John 17:3
Luke 15:11–32
Romans 3:23
Romans 6:23
2 Thessalonians
  1:8–9
1 John 1:5
Romans 5:8
1 Corinthians
  15:3–6
1 Corinthians
  15:56–57
John 1:12
Ephesians 2:8–9
John 3:3
1 John 5:11–13
Hebrews 13:5

CHAPTER 5

John 10:10
John 14:27
John 16:33
John 14:14
John 8:35–36
Revelation 1:5
Philippians 4:13
John 14:12
Matthew 28:18–20
Acts 1:8
John 3:18
1 John 3:2
Philippians 3:21
Romans 6:11–14
Romans 6:22
Psalm 37:5–7
Galatians 5:22–25

CHAPTER 6

2 Corinthians 3:18
Galatians 3:11

Philippians 4:6–7
John 15:4
2 Timothy 3:16–17
John 3:36
John 14:21
Matthew 4:19
Hebrews 11:1
Matthew 6:25–27

CHAPTER 7

John 14:2–4
1 Corinthians
  13:12
Revelation 14:13

CHAPTER 8

Hebrews 11:10,
  13–16
2 Corinthians 5:20
2 Timothy 4:7–8
Matthew 22:37–40
Hebrews 13:8
Matthew 25:21

About the Author

DR. BILL BRIGHT, fueled by his passion to share the love and claims of Jesus Christ with "every living person on earth," was the founder and president of Campus Crusade for Christ. The world's largest Christian ministry, Campus Crusade serves people in 191 countries through a staff of 26,000 full-time employees and more than 225,000 trained volunteers working in some sixty targeted ministries and projects that range from military ministry to inner-city ministry.

Bill Bright was so motivated by what is known as the Great Commission, Christ's command to carry the gospel throughout the world, that in 1956 he wrote a booklet titled *The Four Spiritual Laws*, which has been printed in 200 languages and distributed to more than 2.5 billion people. Other books Bright authored include *Discover the Book God Wrote, God: Discover His Character, Come Help Change Our World, The Holy Spirit: The Key to Supernatural Living, Life Without Equal, Witnessing Without Fear, Coming Revival, Journey Home,* and *Red Sky in the Morning.*

In 1979 Bright commissioned the *JESUS* film, a feature-length dramatization of the life of Christ. To date, the film has been viewed by more than 5.7 billion people in 191 countries and has become the most widely viewed and translated film in history.

Dr. Bright died in July 2003 before the final editing of this book. But he prayed that it would leave a legacy of his love for Jesus and the power of the Holy Spirit to change lives. He is survived by his wife, Vonette; their sons and daughters-in-law; and four grandchildren.

If you have trusted Christ as Savior and Lord
as a result of reading this book,
we would like to hear from you.

We'll put you in touch with the
helpful staff of Dr. Bright's worldwide ministry,
Campus Crusade for Christ International,
who can encourage you in your spiritual journey.

✠ ✠ ✠

Please contact us at
VICTOR BOOKS
Cook Communications Ministries, Dept. 201
4050 Lee Vance View
Colorado Springs, CO 80918

Or visit our Web site: www.cookministries.com

Victor®
The Bible Teacher's Teacher